PERGAMON INSTITUTE OF ENGLISH (OXFORD)

Council of Europe Modern Languages Project

Identifying the Needs
of Adults
Learning a Foreign Language

Other Titles in the Series

OSKARSSON M
Approaches to self-assessment in foreign language learning

TRIM J L M
Developing a unit/credit scheme of adult language learning

TRIM J L M, R RICHTERICH, J A VAN EK, and D A WILKINS
Systems development in adult language learning

VAN EK J A and L G ALEXANDER
Threshold Level English

VAN EK J A, L G ALEXANDER and M A FITZPATRICK
Waystage English

See also
SYSTEM: The International Journal of Educational Technology and Language
Learning Systems. (Free specimen copies available on request.)

The Council of Europe was established by ten nations on 5 May 1949, since when its membership has progressively increased to twenty-one. Its aim is "to achieve a greater unity between its Members for the purpose of safeguarding and realising the ideals and principles which are their common heritage and facilitating their economic and social progress". This aim is pursued by discussion of questions of common concern and by agreements and common action in economic, social, cultural, scientific, legal and administrative matters.

The Council for Cultural Cooperation was set up by the Committee of Ministers of the Council of Europe on 1 January 1962 to draw up proposals for the cultural policy of the Council of Europe, to coordinate and give effect to the overall cultural programme of the organisation and to allocate the resources of the Cultural Fund. All the member governments of the Council of Europe, together with the Holy See and Finland which have acceded to the European Cultural Convention, are represented on the Council for Cultural Cooperation.

The aim of the work carried out by the Council for Cultural Cooperation in the area of modern language learning is to encourage the development of *understanding, cooperation* and *mobility* among Europeans by improving and broadening the learning of *modern languages* by all sections of the population. This aim will be pursued
  — by making generally available the basic tools for the systematic planning, construction and conduct of learning programmes geared to the needs and motivations of the learners and to the changing requirements of society;
  — by helping to prepare teachers to play their proper roles in such programmes,
  — and by further developing a framework for close and effective international cooperation in the promotion of language learning.

For this purpose, and under the authority of the Council for Cultural Cooperation, a number of studies have been prepared, some of which are being published in this Council of European Modern Language Series. However, the opinions expressed in the studies written in this framework are not to be regarded as reflecting the policy of any government, of the Committee of Ministers or the Secretary General of the Council of Europe.

Applications for reproduction and translation should be addressed to the Director of Education, Culture and Sport, Council of Europe, Strasbourg (France).

Identifying the Needs of Adults Learning a Foreign Language

Prepared for the

COUNCIL OF EUROPE

by

RENÉ RICHTERICH
University of Berne

and

JEAN-LOUIS CHANCEREL
University of Neuchâtel

Published for and on behalf of the
COUNCIL OF EUROPE
by

PERGAMON PRESS

OXFORD · NEW YORK · TORONTO · SYDNEY · PARIS · FRANKFURT

U.K.	Pergamon Press Ltd., Headington Hill Hall, Oxford OX3 0BW, England
U.S.A.	Pergamon Press Inc., Maxwell House, Fairview Park, Elmsford, New York 10523, U.S.A.
CANADA	Pergamon of Canada, Suite 104, 150 Consumers Road, Willowdale, Ontario M2J 1P9, Canada
AUSTRALIA	Pergamon Press (Aust.) Pty, Ltd., P.O. Box 544, Potts Point, N.S.W. 2011, Australia
FRANCE	Pergamon Press SARL, 24 rue des Ecoles, 75240 Paris, Cedex 05, France
FEDERAL REPUBLIC OF GERMANY	Pergamon Press GmbH, 6242 Kronberg-Taunus, Pferdstrasse 1, Federal Republic of Germany

First edition 1977

This edition 1980

British Library Cataloguing in Publication Data
Richterich, René
Identifying the needs of adults learning a foreign
language. – (Pergamon Institute of English (Oxford).
Council of Europe language learning series).
1. Language and languages – Study and teaching
2. Adult education
I. Title   II. Chancerel, Jean Louis   III. Series
418′.007   P53   79–42963
ISBN 0–08–024592–7

Printed and bound in Great Britain by
William Clowes (Beccles) Limited, Beccles and London

204076

CONTENTS

	Page
Preface to this edition	vii
Foreword	ix

PART ONE: INTRODUCTION

1. Identifying language needs in a systems approach to the learning of a modern language	3
2. Aims	9
3. Limitations	12
4. Prospects	13

PART TWO: TYPES OF INFORMATION

5. Identification by the learner of his needs	17
I In relation to his resources	17
II In relation to his objectives	20
III In relation to methods of assessment	22
IV In relation to curricula	26
6. Identification of the learner's needs by the teaching establishment	30
V In relation to its resources	30
VI In relation to its objectives	33
VII In relation to its methods of assessment	35
VIII In relation to its syllabuses	39
7. Identification of the learner's needs by the user-institution	43
IX In relation to its resources	43
X In relation to its objectives	44
XI In relation to its methods of assessment	46
XII In relation to its programmes	47
Appendix I: Identifying language needs in four different cases	49

PART THREE: METHODS OF COLLECTION

8. Introduction	53
9. Surveys	55
10. Sample surveys	57
11. Questionnaires	59
Appendix II: Fremdsprachenkentnisse der österreichischen Bevölkerung Personenblatt	62
Appendix III: Etude de la demande de formation en langue étrangère de la population adulte de l'agglomération grenobloise	64
Appendix IV: Questionnaire to graduates	72
12. Interviews	78

Appendix V: Guide d'entretien à l'usage des responsables de formation en
    langues étrangères 80
   13. Attitude scales 81
Appendix VI: French attitude scale 83
Appendix VII: Echelle d'attitude à l'égard de l'apprentissage des langues 84
Appendix VIII: Echelle d'attitude à l'égard de l'espagnol 85
   14. Intelligence tests 86
   15. Language tests 88
   16. Job analysis 90
   17. Content analysis 92
   18. Statistics 93
   19. Determination of objectives 94
Appendix IX: Définir les objectifs de l'éducation 96
Appendix X: The London Chamber of Commerce and Industry 97
Appendix XI: Prospectus des Eurocentres 98

Bibliography 99

PREFACE TO THIS EDITION

From its earliest days, the group of experts charged by the Council for Cultural Cooperation of the Council of Europe with investigating the feasibility of a European unit/credit scheme for foreign language learning by adults envisaged such a scheme as 'learner-centred, needs- and motivation-based.' The paper produced by M Richterich for the 1973 volume *Systems Development in Modern Language Learning* (also published in this series) defined the parameters of language use and language learning according to the strict parallelism required by a situationalist approach. In theory, a programme of needs analysis should have preceded the work on specification of objectives. Considerations of time and money, however, as well of technical difficulty prevented the principle from being put into effect. A valuable enquiry into language use and study was built into the Austrian mini-census programme for 1974. The interesting and to some extent unexpected results of the enquiry have exerted a long-term influence on the planning of language courses in Austria. One lesson which had to be learnt from the mini-census was, however, that the questions asked in such a framework must be few and utterly transparent. An examination of international experience in the conduct of needs surveys (of which a register is kept at CILT,* and of which a compendium of studies is to be made by the Council of Europe) underlines the difficulty of large-scale enquiries. Questionnaires are often difficult to formulate and interpret; logistic difficulties lead to irregularity and biassing of coverage; changes in circumstances may render findings rapidly out-of-date; variation in circumstances makes projection difficult from one group to another, etc.

For these and other reasons, the thinking of the sub-groups on needs and indeed of the Modern Languages Project in general has moved a long way from the notion that needs analysis, consisting simply in predicting the characteristics of future language use, could and should be conducted once and for all in advance of the other stages of course planning. The concept of 'need' has expanded to cover other aspects of the personal and social development of the individual, as well as the development of study skills and of self-reliance as a learner. Course planning must be based not only on the needs – even in this wider sense – of the individual learner, but must take account of the needs of the social groups to which he belongs, the institutions providing the educational framework and the social institutions that provide the resources. In concentrating on needs, we neglect at our peril demands and motivations, which are quite another thing. In fact we must establish as many of the relevant characteristics of all the partners to the learning process as we can, while still focussing on the learners, with their varying experience, age, intelligence, learning styles and expectations as well as needs and motivations. On reflection it is clear that these parameters do not remain constant throughout an extended learning programme. Accordingly, they must be continuously monitored, and a well-designed programme must have the flexibility to respond to changes in the learners, the teachers and the circumstances in which they are working. Some, but by no means all, of these changes can be predicted. For the rest, we must recognize the fact that the ability to monitor change, and to change the learning programme accordingly, is another of the sophisticated skills that are now being required of the teacher. The aim of this publication, as of the others in this series, is to alert teachers, learners and

* Centre for Information on Language Teaching and Research (London).

vii

course designers to the issues involved and to provide them with some of the tools they need to meet the demands made upon them by new styles of systematic, communicative language teaching and learning.

J L M Trim
London, 1980

FOREWORD

This study is part of the work programme of the group of experts appointed by the Council for Cultural Cooperation of the Council of Europe to develop a unit/credit system for learning languages.

Since this system is essentially meant to be centred on the adult learner, the methods firstly of identifying the latter's language needs and secondly of taking account of them in the educational process become the subjects of research, experimentation and application fundamental to the carrying out of the project. It was for this reason that after the St. Wolfgang Symposium of 1973 a working sub-group was set up for the purpose of:

(a) collecting, analyzing and disseminating information on analyzing and identifying language needs;
(b) defining the part played by the identification of needs in the development of unit/credit systems of learning;
(c) suggesting methods of identification;
(d) acting as advisers in connection with the work of experimentation and application.

In a way this study is a summary of the sub-group's deliberations and research, which means that the authors owe a great deal to the various members. Without them the study simply would not have been possible and we would like to thank all of them, and especially Vaughan James and Louis Porcher, very warmly for their collaboration and contributions.

René Richterich, Berne
Jean-Louis Chancerel, Neuchâtel
Switzerland
1977

PART ONE: INTRODUCTION

1. IDENTIFYING LANGUAGE NEEDS IN A SYSTEMS APPROACH TO THE LEARNING OF A MODERN LANGUAGE

System(s) and systemic approach

In trying to describe the component elements of a European unit/credit system for the learning of modern languages and the way in which it works, and to facilitate the introduction of such a system (which since 1971 has been the task of the group of experts and its sub-groups working for the Council of Europe), we find ourselves constantly subjected to conflicting pressures. How are we to define certain indispensable, theoretical fundamentals whilst at the same time meeting the pressing demand for ready-made recipes for dealing with the practical and immediate application of the system? How are we to develop a general system which must necessarily impose certain restraints but which must be capable of operating, without losing any of its coherence or originality, under all special educational, political, economic and institutional conditions? How is it possible to suggest a system inevitably involving essential alterations to existing institutions and at the same time take into account their constitutional resistance to change? In short, the more the project advances, the more difficult does it become to strike a balance between theory and practice, between the general and the special, between medium or long-term aims and those of the immediate future, between restraint and freedom of choice, between change and updating. But perhaps such contradictions should be regarded as inherent to the vigorous growth of a system that is meant to be open and flexible. Thus 'the group of experts set about its task in a systemic manner. It undertook to assist planners and administrators concerned with teaching, teachers and learners – in short, all those involved in language learning – by supplying them with the conceptual tools they need to enable them to make rational, sensible decisions which will have some influence on the language learning process.' (Trim, J L M, preface to the publication by Coste, D *et al* (1976) *Un niveau-seuil,* Strasbourg, Council of Europe, p iii). Thus the work done as part of this project is not intended to provide a finished product, a system, but the instruments required to construct one. It is up to every user to adapt them to his circumstances and possibilities. For this reason the term 'systemic approach' seems to us to be more suitable than that of 'system' hitherto employed, even if the different elements of which the latter is composed have been described and organized so as to form a coherent, structured whole. For no system of learning can exist except through experience of its institutional functioning, and it is only in relation to that experience that its various elements can be introduced. On the other hand the first term seems to us to fit in better with the aims we seek to achieve since it does not presuppose the existence of a finished system but merely the means of producing one. 'A systemic approach is not the answer to a problem but it does represent a rational, scientific means of finding the best answer. It is a well designed procedure, structured so as to minimize preconceived opinions and maximize the objectivity necessary in order to find a reliable scientific solution to a problem.' (*Systèmes multimedia dans l'éducation des adultes,* Internationales Zentralinstitut für das

Jugend- und Bildungsfernsehen, Munich, 1971, quoted by Galisson, R, and D Coste (1976) *Dictionnaire de didactique des langues*, Hachette, Paris, p. 552). We can make use of this definition for our own purposes if we cut out the two uses of the adjective 'scientific' which, in the present state of our knowledge about language learning, could only be excessive.

There are several documents describing the development of this approach (*cf Systems Development in Adult Language Learning,** Council of Europe, Strasbourg, 1973; articles in No 28 of the periodical *Education and Culture,* Council of Europe, Strasbourg, 1975; van Ek, J, (1975) *The Threshold Level,** Council of Europe, Strasbourg, Coste, D, *et al* (1976) *Un niveau-seuil,* Council of Europe, Strasbourg, various mimeographed documents produced by the Council of Europe, such as the general reports by J L M Trim, Project Director), and in order that we may better illustrate the part played by the identification of language needs we shall confine ourselves here to summarizing the essential elements and relationships in the following diagram:

Figure 1

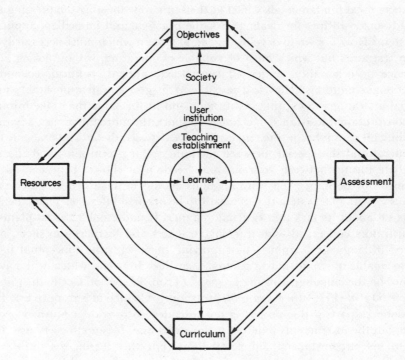

An approach centred on the learner

We see that the learner occupies the central position in this figure. Everything starts from him and everything goes back to him. It is not merely in relation to him, but with him, and depending on his resources (time, available cash, personality, etc.) that his learning objectives will be defined, that the methods of judging when and how they have been attained will be selected, and that a curriculum of learning (by curriculum we understand all the means employed to attain the objectives: teacher, teaching materials, technical aids, methods, timetable etc.) will be made available to

* Published also by Pergamon Press, 1980, in series with the present volume.

4

him. If there is one desirable feature insisted on from the outset, it is that the system should be centred on the learner. But the latter runs the risk of being regarded as an entity whose personality, aspirations and needs will indeed be taken into account but only insofar as they coincide with the aims and image adopted by the teaching establishments and utilizing institutions in which he is involved. Thus the learner may well seem to be at the centre, but it is not he who has put himself there, but the system. The 'centering', if it is to be more than an educational illusion, can but pass through the definition of various forms of participation. 'The act of learning rests with the person who learns', it is true, but the latter is never on his own. To arrive at the act he must necessarily go through a teaching establishment which, in turn will be dependent, either directly or indirectly, on utilizing institutions, and these again necessarily operate in a particular society. Interdependence is therefore close. And if a learner wishes to choose learning objectives, methods of assessment and a curriculum that is in accordance with his resources, he will be able to do so only subject to pressures and influences brought to bear by establishments and institutions and by society. Even the self-taught student will be subject to them by reason of the material he has chosen. The thing that needs to be defined in a systemic approach to language learning intended to be centred on the learner is his freedom of choice. The things that need to be incorporated into systems constructed in accordance with that approach are the means of contributing, discussing, negotiating and participating which will really enable him to centre his learning on himself, but within an institutional framework. It will thus necessarily be vital to seek a compromise between the resources, objectives, methods of assessment and curricula thought of by the learner, and the resources, objectives, methods of assessment and curricula which the teaching establishments, user-institutions and society have more or less clearly defined for themselves.

Part played by the identification of language needs

At the present stage of our work we believe that the identification of language needs is the most favourable means, though there may be others, of seeking this compromise and deciding on the methods of contributing, discussing, negotiating and participating as between learner and teaching establishments and/or user-institutions. If it does not appear in our diagram illustrating the systemic approach, this is because it does not form a specific element of it but pervades it all the time, in all directions and at all levels. It is realized that the construction of a unit/credit system for learning modern languages presupposes analysis and identification of needs.

'Quite obviously it will be found that the introduction of a unit/credit system of this nature presupposes that a number of stages have been completed:

(a) the language needs have been analyzed.
(b) Based on consideration of these different needs, learning objectives have been selected and precisely defined.' etc (Coste, D, *et al* (1976) *Un niveau-seuil* Council of Europe, Strasbourg, p. 12).

'It is also evident that the success of the undertaking is closely dependent on the correctness of a number of important assumptions that control the whole system, for example:

It is possible to express or describe language needs precisely.

These needs can be translated – or at any rate – integrated – into the definition of learning objectives which are themselves clearly formulated.' etc (*op cit*, p 13)

5

At the present time, on the contrary, we would rather incline to the opinion that the identification of needs ought not to be a preliminary step in the construction of systems since it ought to be possible for it to take place at any time, at different levels and with variable degrees of precision and clearness. Instead of being an analytical procedure, it should rather be a didactic measure (just as imperfect and relative as all others), an integral part of the learning systems themselves to be used by the learner and the institutions to enable them to:

(a) appreciate, with varying degrees of explicitness depending upon requirements and possibilities, certain factors and data capable of influencing either the point at which learning starts or the learning itself;

(b) define the roles to be played by each party in making decisions about the choice of objectives, methods of assessment and curricula in conformity with the available resources.

Instead of being an occasional feature, as it has tended to be, the identification of language needs becomes a permanent one.

Instead of being descriptive and analytical, it amounts to an appreciation, by all parties concerned, of certain facts and phenomena.

Instead of being static, it becomes a dynamic means of making choices and decisions.

Instead of being uniform, it becomes multiform.

For as Louis Porcher points out,

'need is not a thing that exists and might be encountered ready-made on the street. It is a thing that is constructed, the centre of conceptual networks and the product of a number of epistemological choices (which are not innocent themselves, of course). This obviously does not mean that, at an empirical level, needs, expectations, demands, etc do not exist and are not experienced. It simply means that, in order that they may really be taken into account (particularly at an educational level, in the case of language needs), it is essential that a 'recognition grid', a tool for identifying the empirical, should be developed in advance'. (Porcher, L, *Une notion ambiguë: les 'besoins langagiers'* (linguistique, sociologie, pédagogie), in *Les Cahiers du CRELEF*, No 3, 1977, p 6).

In the same connection Michel Rousson proposes

'the following provisional definition of need: need could be regarded as the expression of a project (whether or not realistic, whether explicit or implicit) of a social agent (individual or collective) *vis-à-vis* a necessity stemming from the agent's relationship with the social environment. This project may be onerous and conflict with other projects'. (Rousson, M, *The concept of need*, in: Chancerel, J-L *et al, Adult education "needs" – methods of identifying them,* Council of Europe, Strasbourg, mimeographed CCC/EES (75) 20, p 3; for anything relating to a theoretical sketch of the concept of need we refer readers to that document).

and again:

'Any project may conflict with other projects of the agent in question or of other agents. This fact therefore implies the existence of continual tension, and hence compromises. But any compromise is temporary. It is therefore safe to say that the fulfilment, the satisfaction of a need implies making a choice, renouncing and negotiating.' (*op cit*, p 4).

From what precedes we see that since needs are not ready-made things it would be very difficult to analyze them, describe them and define them as such. For this reason, identifying them in a systemic approach centred on the learner would necessarily consist of constructing, with him, a learning project and finding, with him, the compromise by means of which he could institutionally and socially fulfil it. In practice this will consist in collecting, processing and using a certain amount of information which should enable the learner to find his feet *vis-à-vis* institutions and society. If we look at the diagram suggested earlier, we shall find that this information can be collected at different levels, in relation to different fields, with varying degrees of precision and at different times, eg:

— information collected by the learner regarding himself, before the course starts, so that he may know what are his resources, what are the objectives he wishes to attain, what methods of assessment he wishes to see used, which curricula he considers best adapted to his resources, objectives and methods of assessment; in most cases this information will be vague, but it will nevertheless be an important element in the creation of awareness on his part. In addition, it may be imagined that in unit/credit systems for the learning of languages, learners may be supplied with identifying instruments enabling them to make this information more precise;

— information collected by the learner regarding himself, during the course, in order to ascertain whether his resources are in line with the course he is following, whether it will enable him to attain the objectives he has set for himself and whether the methods of assessment used enable him to judge his progress; it should be the job of the teaching establishment to provide him with means of obtaining this information. Here some part is played by discussion and negotiation between learner, teacher and establishment in arriving at a compromise regarding the use of resources, methods of assessment, curricula and the definition of the objectives laid down for each of them;

— information on teaching establishments obtained by the learner before the course starts to enable him to select the one most suited to his resources and his ideas of what are his objectives, methods of assessment and curricula; although such information is most often derived from advertisements, one could imagine that the systems will offer a more advanced service or guidance facilities;

— information collected by the teaching establishments regarding themselves to enable them to determine what means they have of adapting their resources, objectives, methods of assessment and curricula to the expectations and require-ments of the learner, before and during the course;

— information on the learner collected by a teaching establishment before the course starts so that, in consultation with him, the establishment can determine what his objectives are and suggest curricula and methods of assessment appropriate to his resources;

— information on the learner collected by a teaching establishment during the course to define possibilities of adaptation and compromise; in this connection we must emphasize that the learner's needs will certainly change whilst he is learning, if only because he will have realized a certain number of facts more clearly; it is therefore essential not only for the establishment and the learner to identify needs jointly as the course proceeds but also, and most important of all, for them to seek fresh compromises periodically;

— information obtained by or in a user-institution, giving a better understanding of the real use of foreign languages (objectives), defining requirements (methods of assessment) and deciding how much weight it attaches to the training (resources and curricula);

— information gathered in a given society so as to make it possible to take stock of its nationals' knowledge and use of foreign languages, its requirements (objectives and methods of assessment) and learning facilities (resources and curricula).

The outcome of the identification of needs will thus be the product of a certain amount of information collected at different levels and times, the amount and the manner of collecting it depending, on the one hand, on requirements and the desire to take account of them felt by individuals and establishments and institutions and, on the other hand, on the means and instruments available. Thus, depending on circumstances, learner and establishment will organize their own methods of identification on the basis of the information which they deem important. In some cases a vague, general overall inquiry will be sufficient, in others analysis, surveys and detailed samplings will be necessary, the main points being:

- that learner and establishment become aware of certain facts and data involved in the learning/teaching of a second language;

- that this realization should lead to discussion, negotiation and participation between the persons concerned with the aim of finding the compromises necessary for the carrying out of any training and without which satisfaction of individual and collective needs can only be illusory.

2. AIMS

By means of this study we have sought to achieve three aims:

1. to show that analysis or identification of language needs ought to be an integral part of the unit/credit language learning processes;
2. to show that all parts of the system are interdependent: analysis of resources and motivations, definition of objectives and methods of assessment, choice of methodologies and teaching curricula;
3. to suggest conceptual instruments for carrying out this identification.

We are addressing a broad range of readers who should be able to use the study at different levels and for different purposes;

– the learner, to awaken his awareness;
– the teacher, to give him a better understanding of the makeup of a group of learners and adapt his teaching accordingly;
– the producer of the material so that he may adapt it to specific categories of learners and include means of identifying needs;
– administrative and teaching executives in establishments to enable them to plan and adapt learning systems.

At this stage we may once again remind ourselves of some facts governing the whole of our approach, especially as regards the third and fourth parts of the study:

Part three: Types of information

– Needs are not fully-developed facts capable of being described in the same way as a house, for example. They are built up by the individual or a group of individuals from an actual complex experience. They are in consequence, variable, multiform and intangible. To identify them would entail gathering a certain amount of information concerning this experience, becoming aware of certain facts and translating them into a more or less precise expression.

– Systems of learning centred on the learner cannot be built up other than with the latter's help and this means that they can operate only through discussion, participation and negotiation.

– But the learner never learns in isolation. Teaching establishments, user-institutions and society all exercise pressures at different levels on his learning or his desire to learn. He can therefore only express his needs through them.

– Since by their nature these needs develop and change in line with actual experience, identifying them must be a continuous process. It becomes one educational means, among others, used for the purpose of discussion, participation and negotiation.

We have summarized the whole of our approach in *Figure 1*. Through it we have established a classification of the types of information that can be collected in order to build up, jointly with the learner, an expression of his needs. This will give us the following broad categories:

Identification of his needs *by the learner*, before and during the course, depending on:

I.   his resources;
II. his objectives;
III. the methods of assessment;
IV. the curricula.

Identification of the learner's needs *by the teaching establishment*, before and during the course, depending on:

I.   its resources;
II. its objectives;
III. its methods of assessment;
IV. its curricula.

Identification of the learner's needs *by the user-institution*, before the course, depending on:

I.   its resources;
II. its objectives;
III. its methods of assessment;
IV. its curricula.

There is a short introduction to each category and for each of them we give a certain amount of information. In addition we suggest some ways and means of collecting the information. Anyone using this part can first read through it quickly, confining himself to the introductions. After that he will pick out the information he thinks essential depending on his opportunities and the level of expression he wishes to attain.

In an appendix to this part we illustrate the identification of language needs applicable to four different circumstances.

Case 1: A person wants to learn English, enrolls at a teaching establishment and learns there.
Case 2: A person wants to learn German and is learning it by self-tuition merely for pleasure.
Case 3: A teaching establishment wants to organize and adapt its methods of teaching French to fit in with the demand.
Case 4: A user-institution has decided to give its commercial executives a knowledge of Spanish to enable them to canvass the markets of certain South American countries.

We should emphasize that these four instances are purely hypothetical and we have made this simulated test solely with the object of finding out what sort of information would appear to us, at first sight and for each case, to be essential or merely desirable. We have confined ourselves to types of information, leaving the reader free to decide what particular information is appropriate to his own situation.

Part four: Means of collection

This contains a brief description in a logical order, proceeding from the general to the particular, of the main methods of collecting information, wherever possible with one or two examples of how they are applied:

1. Surveys
2. Sample surveys
3. Questionnaires
4. Interviews
5. Attitude scales
6. Intelligence tests
7. Language tests
8. Job analysis
9. Content analysis
10. Statistical analysis
11. Fixing of objectives.

Each method will be described in accordance with the following outline:

1. Definition
2. Principles and classification
3. Principles of construction
4. Application.

The examples we have chosen must obviously be reinstated in the context in which they are to be used. This description is completed by a concise bibliography.

3. LIMITATIONS

In endeavouring to achieve the three aims of this study we have once more come up against contradictions between theory and practice, as pointed out previously. Some readers or users of this work will once more fail to find what they were looking for – it will be not sufficiently theoretical, over-simple; not sufficiently practical, too abstract. Not for the purpose of justifying our deficiencies but simply to show clearly what we have been unable to achieve, for various reasons, within the framework of a study of this kind, we would like to draw attention here to some of these limitations:

– The first part does not contain a complete description of a systemic approach to language learning by adults in the shape of a unit/credit system. We have only outlined the part played by identification of language needs in such an approach.
– In the third part we have abandoned the attempt to describe identification of the learner's needs by society because the context seemed to us to be too vast for the potential users of this study.
– The different information mentioned does not, in any case, represent questions that can be included in a questionnaire. In order to be able to do this they would require to be turned into genuine questions in accordance with the rules of construction.
– Each list is open-ended, which means that everyone can add or delete information according to requirements. We make no claim to being exhaustive.
– Some of the lists include information which is mutually exclusive and a choice will therefore have to be made; others give information that is non-exclusive and may thus be complementary.
– In the simulated identification of the four cases set out at the end of the third part we have had to confine ourselves to mentioning types of information without going into details regarding each of them.
– In the last part we have illustrated the various methods of collection by a brief description. Obviously anyone wishing to make use of them will need more detailed information.
– The examples quoted are illustrative only and not qualitative models.
– Lastly, the bibliography also is a concise one. We have mentioned works that we knew well and which we had at hand. The bibliography is therefore a personal one and does not claim to cover the subject fully.

4. PROSPECTS

Any project for the promotion of unit/credit systems for language learning by adults as vast as that of the Council of Europe develops, changes and is adapted from one year to another. It is therefore difficult to say what may happen in the long term. However, the Working Party on the Analysis of Language Needs would like to resume its work and experiments in this field, after the appearance of this study, by embarking on the following activities:

1. There are a number of very interesting and instructive surveys and analyses on the subject of language needs. It would be advisable to read through them systematically to begin with in order to:

    (a) draw up a careful, critical description of them;
    (b) prepare an inventory of the types of information collected in each of them and of the ways in which it is dealt with;
    (c) deduce the methods of collection used and the way of applying them;
    (d) decide what place they occupy in relation to the approach proposed in this study (what defects are there, what has already been applied?);
    (e) see what practical results have been achieved in the teaching of modern languages in the context of these surveys and analyses.

2. We cannot too often repeat that a study such as this cannot be anything other than a more or less theoretical general reference outline to be adapted by every user in accordance with his resources and the objectives he wishes to achieve by identifying his language needs. This outline can become practical and operational only insofar as it is actually applied and adapted to various possible situations. This means that the various aspects of it must be tried out and tested in the field. For this purpose we suggest the following experiments:

    (a) a check made jointly with a number of isolated learners on the different possible methods of identifying their needs themselves before and during the course (self-tuition students and learners in a teaching establishment);

    (b) a check made jointly with several groups of learners on the different possible methods of identifying their needs in certain kinds of teaching establishment before and during the course (self-study circles in Sweden, Eurocentres, Volkshochschulen etc);

    (c) a study in collaboration with a number of teaching establishments of the introduction of administrative and educational organization structures needed for taking account, in their systems, of the needs of learners before and during the courses at the following levels:
    – the establishment generally;
    – the teaching material;
    – teacher training
    (Training centres run by certain user-institutions such as the Civil Service, Eurocentres, Volkshochschulen, Ford, IBM etc);

    (d) identification of the language needs of certain user-institutions such as the medical service, government departments, IBM, Ford, etc.

3. Based on the practical knowledge and experience gained from the work referred to in items 1 and 2, monographs should be published describing various special or general aspects of the identification of language needs, eg:

(a) descriptions of experiments, tests and applications as suggested in items 2 (a)–(d), which descriptions could be used as practical guides for identifying needs, to assist the learners and establishments or institutions in question;

(b) practical descriptions of the actual introduction and use of some methods of collecting and dealing with information in general or particular situations (questionnaires, interviews, attitude scales etc);

(c) descriptions of some methodological applications used in identifying language needs (negotiation, definition of objectives, incorporation into teaching material etc).

4. As this study is only a starting point intended to assign to the identification of language needs its proper place in unit/credit systems in general for language learning, it would be advisable that it should be adapted, completed, changed and brought up to date in line with the experiments and other work done in connection with the project (pilot experiments, research by threshold-level groups, assessment, methodology etc). Provision should therefore be made for periodical publications, making summaries in specific situations of problems connected with the identification of language needs.

PART TWO:
TYPES OF INFORMATION

5. IDENTIFICATION BY THE LEARNER OF HIS NEEDS

I. Identification by the learner of his needs in relation to his resources

I.B Before the course

When a person wishes to learn a foreign language, has decided to or is about to start doing so, it is advisable that he himself should form an idea of the amount of time and money at his disposal and the place where the learning might be done.

In the main the choice of the type of instruction and teaching establishment will depend on these three factors. Besides this, certain details about his identity are invariably essential. But the future learner should also become aware of certain characteristics of his own personality that may play an important part in determining his behaviour and methods of learning.

Most of this information can be compiled by the learner himself without any need for using complicated methods; nevertheless, it might be advisable for him to consult a teaching establishment or advisory service, especially with regard to the becoming aware of his personality. It is possible also that the material required to help the potential learner to collect this sort of information could be made available to him through teaching systems so as to enable him to make his decisions with full knowledge of all the facts. At the present time this is generally done by means of written or visual advertisements or by word of mouth.

Types of information

T.1. Learner's identity

T.1.1.	Age
T.1.2.	Sex
T.1.3.	Marital status
T.1.4.	Number of children
T.1.5.	Nationality
T.1.6.	Address
T.1.7.	Religion
T.1.8.	Number of brothers and sisters
T.1.9.	Occupation of father and mother
T.1.10.	Schooling – General, vocational, specialized (number of years)
T.1.11.	Certificates and diplomas
T.1.12.	Present occupation (eg engineer)
T.1.13.	Present position (eg sales manager)
T.1.14.	Previous occupations
T.1.15.	Previous positions held
T.1.16.	Place of work
T.1.16.1.	Geographical location
T.1.16.2.	Type of firm
T.1.17.	Leisure-time pursuits and hobbies
T.1.18.	Outside activities (politics, arts, clubs, etc)

T.2.1. Personality traits (reserved/frank, timid/venturesome, introvert/extrovert, trusting/suspicious, etc)
T.2.2. Capability (intelligence, memory, ability to learn, etc)
T.2.3. Attitude (positive/negative to language learning in general, to a particular language, to its culture, to its civilization, to the people speaking it, etc)

T.3. Time at learner's disposal
T.3.1.   Number of hours a day
T.3.2.   Number of hours a week
T.3.3.   Number of weeks a month
T.3.4.   Number of months a year
T.3.5.   Number of years
T.3.6.   At what time of day?
T.3.7.   On which days of the week?
T.3.8.   At what time in private life (holidays, free time)?
T.3.9.   At what time in working life (during working hours, free time)?
T.3.10. Learning during working hours
T.3.11. Learning outside working hours

T.4. Where learning is done
T.4.1. In the place where the learner lives
T.4.2. In a place near where he lives
T.4.3. In another place but in the same country
T.4.4. In a country where the language is spoken
T.4.5. In a teaching establishment
T.4.6. At the place of work
T.4.7. Near the place of work
T.4.8. At home

T.5. Financing of tuition
T.5.1.   Paid leave from work
T.5.2.   Partially paid leave from work
T.5.3.   Unpaid leave from work
T.5.4.   All tuition paid for by the establishment where the future learner will use his knowledge
T.5.5.   Tuition partly paid for by the establishment where the future learner will use his knowledge
T.5.6.   Tuition paid for entirely by the future learner
T.5.7.   Tuition paid for entirely by a third party (eg parents)
T.5.8.   Tuiton paid for partly by a third party
T.5.9.   Cost of tuition
T.5.9.1. Course fee
T.5.9.2. Materials and equipment
T.5.9.3. Travelling expenses
T.5.9.4. Cost of board
T.5.9.5. Pocket money
T.5.9.6. Loss of wages
T.5.10. Need to obtain a loan
T.5.11. Possibility of obtaining a grant

Possible steps to be taken by the learner
S.1.   Consulting a person who has had experience of a given type of course
S.2.   Consulting a person who has had experience of learning modern languages
S.3.   Paying attention to the publicity materials of teaching establishments
S.4.   Consulting one or more teaching establishment
S.5.   Consulting an advisory service
S.6.   Consulting third parties (eg parents)
S.7.   Consulting the personnel department of an establishment where the knowledge is to be used
S.8.   Consulting superiors at an establishment where the knowledge is to be used

Means of obtaining information
M.1.   Questionnaires
M.2.   Personality tests
M.3.   Aptitude tests
M.4.   Attitude scales
M.5.   Interviews

I.D During the course

The information the learner has obtained and the ideas he has formed concerning his resources before starting to learn a language will be compared by him, whilst the course continues, with any changes that may take place in his identity and personality, his available time and money and his opportunities for travel. Some of these changes may have a decisive influence on the continuation of his course and cause him to make other decisions than the original ones. Discussion and negotiation will then have to be entered into with the teaching establishment to find out what are the possibilities for adaptation and for arriving at fresh compromises. If the learner is able to obtain most of this information himself, it may be that the teaching material itself will provide him with some of the means for doing so and that the establishment will look into the question of resources with him periodically.

Types of information

T.1.   Learner's identity

Have there been any changes likely to affect the course?

T.1.1.   Marital status
T.1.2.   Address
T.1.3.   Present occupation
T.1.4.   Present position held
T.1.5.   Place of work
T.1.6.   Leisure-time pursuits and hobbies
T.1.7.   Outside activities

T.2.   Learner's personality

Is the information regarding his personality confirmed and what is its influence on the course?

T.2.1.   Personality traits
T.2.2.   Capability
T.2.3.   Attitude

T.3.   Time at learner's disposal

Is the amount of time available still the same?

T.3.1.
   to   *cf* I.B, T.3.
T.3.14.

T.4.   Where learning is done

Is there any reason to change the place?

T.4.1.
   to   *cf* I.B, T.4.
T.4.7.

T.5.   Financing of tuition

Are his financial resources still the same?

T.5.1.
   to   *cf* I.B, T.5.
T.5.11.

Possible steps to be taken by the learner

S.1.   Negotiations with teaching establishment
S.2.   Negotiations with personnel department of the establishment where the knowledge is to be used
S.3.   Negotiations with the superiors at an establishment where the knowledge is to be used
S.4.   Negotiations with a third party

Means of obtaining information

M.1.   Questionnaires
M.2.   Personality tests
M.3.   Aptitude tests
M.4.   Attitude scales
M.5.   Interviews

II. Identification by the learner of his needs in relation to his objectives

II.B Before the course

In most cases the future learner has only a very vague idea of the objectives he would like to achieve by learning a foreign language and, above all, he is unable to specify them. However, this should not prevent him from realizing just how precisely he is capable of thinking out those objectives and then asking himself questions about the spheres in which he proposes to use the second language, the types of use he envisages and the skills he will need to acquire. Even if his description of his objectives does not get beyond nebulous fancies and vague plans, it will nevertheless play an important part in the choice of a course. Here too the future learner ought to be assisted by the provision of means enabling him to become more aware, which is intimately and directly related to the identification of needs in relation to resources and to methods of assessment.

Types of information

T.1.   Level of description of objectives

T.1.1.   In general terms
T.1.2.   In exact operational terms

T.2.   Areas in which the language is intended to be used

T.2.1.   Working life
T.2.2.   Private life (social contacts, cultural interests, etc)

T.3.   Ways in which the language is intended to be used

T.3.1.   Language activities (eg telephoning, negotiating, writing letters)
T.3.2.   Language functions (eg asking for information, giving orders, arguing, explaining)
T.3.3.   Language situations (eg face to face, in a working group)
T.3.4.   Referential objects (eg everyday communications, scientific references)

T.4.   Language skills to be developed

T.4.1.   Understanding speech
T.4.2.   Understanding written matter
T.4.3.   Speaking
T.4.4.   Writing

Possible steps to be taken by the learner

S.1.   Consulting prospectuses issued by teaching establishments
S.2.   Consulting the syllabuses of teaching establishments
S.3.   Consulting lists of objectives prepared in advance
S.4.   Applying to one or more teaching establishments
S.5.   Applying to an advisory service

Means of obtaining information

M.1.   Questionnaires
M.2.   Interviews
M.3.   Lists of language activities, functions and situations prepared in advance

II.D During the course

It may be supposed that the learner's vague ideas about his objectives will alter and become clearer as the course proceeds. The very fact of learning a modern language will, indirectly, alter his first idea. But the teaching establishment will be able to give him direct assistance in appreciating such changes by incorporating in its instructional material instruments enabling the learner to describe ever more clearly the aims of each unit of learning. This means that the teacher must have the professional skill and institutional facilities for taking these changes into consideration and adapting his teaching accordingly.

Types of information

T.1.   Level of description of objectives

T.1.1.   Long-term objectives
T.1.1.1.   General objectives
T.1.1.2.   Operational objectives
T.1.2.   Short-term objectives
T.1.2.1.   General objectives
T.1.2.2.   Operational objectives

T.2.   Changes in areas in which the language is intended to be used

  cf II.B, T.2.

T.3.   Changes in ways in which the language is intended to be used

  cf II.B, T.3.

T.4.   Changes in language skills to be developed

  cf II.B, T.4.

Possible steps to be taken by the learner

S.1.   Learning to define learning objectives
S.2.   Agreeing the necessary adaptations with teacher and teaching establishment

Means of obtaining information

M.1.   Questionnaires
M.2.   Interviews
M.3.   Lists of language activities, functions and situations prepared in advance
M.4.   Methods of defining objectives

III. Identification by the learner of his needs in relation to methods of assessment

III.B Before the course

Definition of objectives and definition of the methods of checking and assessing how they are to be attained cannot be separated. The future learner will first take into account the information given in his language background and try to evaluate his previous knowledge of the language he intends to learn. Even if this assessment is vague and subjective, it is nonetheless important since it reflects his idea of what he has accomplished, an idea that it is essential to know about because it will persist throughout the course. The next essential is for the future learner to decide what sort of qualification he wishes or is required to obtain.

Types of information

T.1.   Learner's language background

T.1.1.	Native tongue(s)
T.1.2.	Father's native tongue(s)
T.1.3.	Mother's native tongue(s)
T.1.4.	Foreign languages known
T.1.5.	Foreign languages learnt
T.1.6.	Time when languages were learnt
T.1.6.1.	Before schooldays
T.1.6.2.	At school
T.1.6.3.	After completion of schooling
T.1.7.	Length of this course
T.1.7.1.	Number of weeks, months or years
T.1.7.2.	Number of hours a week
T.1.7.3.	How long is it since the learner was last learning a language?
T.1.8.	Types of courses
T.1.8.1.	Language courses without audio-visual aids or language laboratory
T.1.8.2.	Audio-visual language courses with language laboratory
T.1.8.3.	Audio-visual language courses without language laboratory
T.1.8.4.	Individual study without any particular method
T.1.8.5.	Individual study by self-tuition method
T.1.8.6.	Radio or television language courses
T.1.8.7.	Crash course
T.1.8.8.	Suggestopaedia
T.1.8.9.	Large group (over ten learners)
T.1.8.10	Small group (less than ten learners)
T.1.9.	Where learning is done
T.1.9.1.	Compulsory school
T.1.9.2.	Vocational school
T.1.9.3.	University
T.1.9.4.	Language centre attached to a university
T.1.9.5.	School specializing in teaching foreign languages
T.1.9.6.	Training centre run by a firm or other institution needing language knowledge
T.1.9.7.	Official or semi-official permanent education establishment
T.1.9.8.	Outside the country where the language is spoken
T.1.9.9.	In the country where the language is spoken
T.1.9.10	At home
T.1.10.	Types of qualification obtained for languages learnt
T.1.11.	Use made of languages learnt
T.1.11.1.	Oral

T.1.11.1.1.	Frequently
T.1.11.1.2.	Occasionally
T.1.11.1.3.	Never
T.1.11.2.	Written
T.1.11.2.1.	Frequently
T.1.11.2.2.	Occasionally
T.1.11.2.3.	Never
T.1.11.3.	In working and public life
T.1.11.4.	In private life
T.1.11.5.	In the country where the language is spoken
T.1.11.6.	Outside the country where the language is spoken
T.1.12.	Courses at present being taken in one or more languages besides the one contemplated
T.1.12.1.	Length of course(s)
T.1.12.2.	Type of course
T.1.12.3.	Where course(s) is/are being taken

T.2. Assessment of level attained in language contemplated

T.2.1.	Understanding of speech
T.2.2.	Understanding of writing
T.2.3.	Speaking
T.2.4.	Writing

T.3. Type of qualifications aimed at

T.3.1.	Diploma of an official establishment
T.3.2.	Diploma of a semi-official establishment
T.3.3.	Diploma of a non-official establishment
T.3.4.	Testimonial
T.3.5.	Certificate
T.3.6.	None

T.4. Purpose of qualification aimed at

| T.4.1. | Professional or vocational |
| T.4.2. | Cultural |

Possible steps to be taken by the learner

S.1.	Compilation of data on his own language background
S.2.	Obtaining information on types of qualification available
S.3.	Getting information on requirements for obtaining the various types of qualification
S.4.	Applying to one or more teaching establishments
S.5.	Applying to an advisory service
S.6.	Applying to someone with experience of assessment problems

Means of obtaining information

M.1.	Questionnaires
M.2.	Placement tests
M.3.	Aptitude tests

24

III.D During the course

Throughout the whole of his course, the learner ought to be able to check his progress and compare his newly acquired knowledge with his ideas concerning his previous knowledge. Constant encouragement of this kind is recognized as an important factor in motivation. The terms and content of such continuous assessment and the conditions for obtaining a final qualification should be defined jointly with his teacher and the teaching establishment. Just as with the specification of objectives, assessment should be an integral part of the learning material and should be carried out at two levels – general and operational. This will also help the learner to appreciate his own strategies.

Types of information

T.1.   Conditions of assessment

T.1.1.   Objective assessment from outside
T.1.2.   Subjective assessment from outside
T.1.3.   Guided self-assessment
T.1.4.   Subjective self-assessment
T.1.5.   Continuous assessment
T.1.6.   Periodical assessment
T.1.7.   Single assessment
T.1.8.   Individual assessment
T.1.9.   Assessment in groups
T.1.10.   Assessment criteria
T.1.10.1.   Marks
T.1.10.2.   Appraisal of general progress

T.2.   Types of assessment

T.2.1.   Objective tests
T.2.2.   Self-assessment
T.2.3.   Check exercises
T.2.4.   Homework
T.2.5.   Examinations
T.2.6.   Alternation of educational assessment and actual use of the language

T.3.   Level of assessment

T.3.1.   Assessment of general objectives
T.3.2.   Assessment of operational objectives

T.4.   Content of assessment

T.4.1.   Phonetics
T.4.2.   Morphology
T.4.3.   Syntax
T.4.4.   Lexis
T.4.5.   Language activities
T.4.6.   Language functions
T.4.7.   Language situations
T.4.8.   Referential objects
T.4.9.   Understanding of speech

T.4.10. Understanding of written matter
T.4.11. Speaking
T.4.12. Writing
T.4.13. General content (eg textbooks, methods, threshold-levels).

Possible steps to be taken by the learner

S.1. Self-observation during course
S.2. Becoming aware of own learning strategies
S.3. Discussion of methods of assessment with teacher and teaching establishment

Means of obtaining information

M.1. Progress tests
M.2. Examination tests
M.3. Self-assessment

IV. Identification by the learner of his needs in relation to curricula

IV.B Before the course

The future learner will have chosen his course in accordance with his resources, his more or less clearly defined objectives and the methods of assessment he would like to have applied to him. The more information on these three matters he has collected, the clearer will be his awareness of his needs and the better able he will be to make his choice. In order that systems really centred on the learner may operate properly, it seems that neutral advisory services should be set up whose role would be to help the learner obtain information about his needs and to advise him about possible courses. At the present time it appears that he relies too much on the publicity materials of teaching establishments and his impression of how good they are.

It should be remembered that a teaching syllabus represents the implementation of means available for the attainment of objectives fixed by reference to methods of assessment and resources. The idea formed by a future learner will therefore depend on the information he has previously obtained.

Types of information

T.1. Types of establishment

cf V.B, T.1.

T.2. Time taken up by the syllabus

T.2.1. Number of hours a day
T.2.2. Number of days a week
T.2.3. Number of weeks a month
T.2.4. Number of months a year
T.2.5. Number of years
T.2.6. At what time of day

T.2.7. On which days in the week
T.2.8. During holidays

T.3. Where learning is done

cf I.B, T.4.

T.4. Cost of course

T.4.1. Enrolment fee
T.4.2. Cost of course
T.4.3. Cost of materials
T.4.4. Cost of board
T.4.5. Pocket money

T.5. Teacher

T.5.1. Image of teacher
T.5.2. Desired relationship between teacher and learner

T.6. Learners

T.6.1. Number of learners in group
T.6.2. Self-tuition
T.6.3. Desired relationship between learners

T.7. Technical aids to learning

T.7.1. Language laboratory
T.7.2. Television
T.7.3. Radio
T.7.4. Audio-visual aids
T.7.5. Visual aids
T.7.6. Auditive aids
T.7.7. Printed aids
T.7.8. Multi-media

T.8. Areas in which curriculum is used

T.8.1. Working life
T.8.2. Private life

T.9. Content of syllabus

T.9.1. Phonetics
T.9.2. Morphology
T.9.3. Syntax
T.9.4. Lexis
T.9.5. Language activities
T.9.6. Language functions
T.9.7. Language situations
T.9.8. Referential objects

T.10 Skills developed by the course

T.10.1. Understanding of speech
T.10.2. Understanding of written material

T.10.3. Speaking
T.10.4. Writing

T.11. Course level

T.11.1. Beginners
T.11.2. False beginners
T.11.4. Intermediate
T.11.4. Advanced
T.11.5. Further training

T.12. Material used in course

T.12.1. Ideas regarding desired material
T.12.2. Reference to known material

T.13. Course methods

T.13.1. Ideas regarding method desired
T.13.2. Reference to known method

Possible steps to be taken by the learner

S.1. Consulting prospectuses of teaching establishments
S.2. Consulting syllabuses of teaching establishments
S.3. Consulting one or more teaching establishment
S.4. Consulting an advisory service
S.5. Consulting someone with experience of a type of course

Means of obtaining information

M.1. Questionnaires
M.2. Attitude scales
M.3. Interviews

IV.D During the course

The learners' resources may perhaps have altered during the course; or again his objectives may have changed or he may want or have to obtain a different kind of certificate from the one originally chosen. All such possible alterations will have their repercussions on the curriculum taken and the learner must know how he can continue his studies, what are the possibilities offered by the teaching establishment and what fresh compromises he can find there.

Types of information

T.1. Types of establishment

T.1.1. Is it necessary for the learner to move to another establishment for any reason?

T.2. Time needed by the syllabus

T.2.1. Is the timetable chosen still adequate?

28

T.3.   Place where learning is done

T.3.1.   Does the learner need to change to another place for any reason?

T.4.   Cost of course

T.4.1.   Do any changes in financial resources involve an alteration of the syllabus chosen?

T.5.   Teacher

T.5.1.   Should there be a change of teacher for any reason?

T.6.   Learners

T.6.1.   Should the learner change to another group?

T.7.   Technical aids to learning

T.7.1.   Do other objectives call for the use of different technical aids?

T.8.   Areas in which curriculum is used

T.8.1.   Are the original areas of use still valid?

T.9.   Content of syllabus

T.9.1.   Do other objectives or methods of assessment call for changes in content?

T.10.   Skills developed by the syllabus

T.10.1.   Should one skill be developed more or less than another?

T.11.   Course level

T.11.1.   Is a change of level necessary?

T.12.   Material used in course

T.12.1.   Is the material used suitable?

T.13.   Course methods

T.13.1.   Do the method(s) used come up to the learner's expectations?

Possible steps to be taken by the learner

S.1.   Negotiating alterations with the establishment
S.2.   Changing to another establishment

Means of obtaining information

M.1.   Interviews
M.2.   Questionnaires
M.3.   Observations

6. IDENTIFICATION OF THE LEARNER'S NEEDS BY THE TEACHING ESTABLISHMENT

V. Identification of the learner's needs by the teaching establishment in relation to its resources

V.B Before the course

It is extremely advisable for a teaching establishment to improve its knowledge of the needs of future learners. This is a means of developing its policy in line with demand. It is therefore important that the establishment also take stock of its resources so as to find out what possibilities it has of making adjustments and taking the needs of its students into consideration. Acting indirectly in relation to them and directly in collaboration with them it will define its own objectives and the methods of assessing them and suggest suitable curricula. The wider the range it can offer, the more chance it will have of meeting the needs of the greatest number; but the more resources it must have to draw on.

Types of information

T.1.   Types of establishment

T.1.1.   Private establishments providing only language courses for adults
T.1.2.   Private establishments teaching languages among other subjects
T.1.3.   Official or semi-official establishments providing only language courses for adults
T.1.4.   Official or semi-official establishments teaching other subjects besides languages
T.1.5.   Private or public vocational schools offering language courses
T.1.6.   Centres, institutes and research and teaching departments attached to a university and giving language tuition
T.1.7.   Training centres attached to a firm or other establishment where languages are used
T.1.8.   Radio and television services broadcasting language courses
T.1.9.   Firms selling language correspondence courses
T.1.10.   Firms selling self-tuition courses

T.2.   Reputation

T.2.1.   What is the establishment's own idea of itself?
T.2.2.   How is it regarded by outsiders?

T.3.   Staff

T.3.1.   Number of people employed on administrative duties
T.3.2.   Secretariat
T.3.3.   Educational executives
T.3.4.   Educational advisers   ⎫
T.3.5.   Research staff   ⎬ What are their native languages?
T.3.6.   Staff engaged on planning courses ⎭

T.3.7.　Staff engaged on producing courses
T.3.8.　Staff engaged on implementing courses
T.3.9.　Teachers

} What are their native languages?

T.4.　Length of time employed

T.4.1.　　People employed full-time
T.4.2.　　People employed part-time
T.4.3.　　People engaged for one specific job
T.4.4.　　Number of hours per teacher
T.4.5.　　Distribution of courses in time
T.4.5.1.　Extended courses (several hours a week)
T.4.5.2.　Intensive courses (several hours a day)
T.4.5.3.　Courses extending over the full year
T.4.5.4.　Courses confined to a particular time of the year
T.4.5.5.　*'A la carte'* courses
T.4.5.6.　Courses starting at frequent intervals
T.4.5.7.　Courses starting at longer intervals
T.4.6.　　Time devoted to research
T.4.7.　　Time devoted to planning
T.4.8.　　Time devoted to implementing courses
T.4.9.　　Time devoted to producing courses
T.4.10　　Time devoted to guidance work

T.5.　Places and methods of setting up establishments

T.5.1.　　Number of establishments set up
T.5.2.　　Country
T.5.3.　　Region
T.5.4.　　Small places
T.5.5.　　Average-sized town
T.5.6.　　Large towm
T.5.7.　　Correspondence or broadcast courses
T.5.8.　　Type of building
T.5.9.　　Number of rooms for administration
T.5.10.　 Number of rooms for teaching
T.5.11.　 Number of rooms for research
T.5.12.　 Number of rooms for guidance work
T.5.13.　 Types of rooms

T.6.　Number of languages taught

T.7.　Financial arrangements

T.7.1.　　Profit-making establishment
T.7.2.　　Non-profit-making establishment
T.7.3.　　Cost of courses
T.7.4.　　Salaries paid to various types of employees
T.7.5.　　Operational budget
T.7.6.　　Research budget
T.7.7.　　Guidance work budget
T.7.8.　　Planning budget

T.7.9.   Budget devoted to implementing courses
T.7.10.   Budget devoted to production of courses

Possible steps to be taken by the teaching establishment

S.1.   As a general rule teaching establishments do keep this kind of information up to date
S.2.   In order to obtain fuller information they may also consult an organization specializing in institutional analysis.

Means of obtaining information

M.1.   Statistics
M.2.   Questionnaires

V.D During the course

As we have seen, the learner's needs may change during the course. If a teaching establishment wishes to apply a systems approach centred on individuals or groups learning a language there, it must normally be capable of making allowance for these changes and thus altering its resources to suit the new needs. Here we come up against the whole problem of the adaptability and flexibility of institutional structures to which there is usually no solution. However, it is on this factor that success or failure of the possible applications of the systems approach outlined in this study depends.

In order that they may be able to make the necessary decisions enabling them to arrive at new compromises with the learners, teaching establishments must regularly ask themselves a number of questions concerning changes to be made as regards time, place, staff and financial resources.

Types of information

T.1.   Types of establishment

T.1.1.   Should any change be made in the status of the establishment?

T.2.   Reputation

T.2.1.   Is it necessary to bring about any change in the establishment's reputation?
T.2.2.   Is its reputation altering of its own accord?

T.3.   Staff

T.3.1.   Is there any need for changes in the number, jobs and duties of the various classes of people employed at the establishment?

T.4.   Length of time employed

T.4.1.   Is there any need for changes in the time spent on teaching and the time devoted by staff to the establishment's various activities?

T.5.   Place and method of setting up establishment

T.5.1.   Would it be advisable to open other teaching centres or to close down some?

T.6.1.   What effect do decisions made have on financial resources, salaries, budgets and the cost of courses?

Possible steps to be taken by the teaching establishment

S.1.   Decisions taken after analysis of demand from a given section of the population
S.2.   Negotiation with learners
S.3.   Fresh advertising
S.4.   Introduction of flexible, adaptable structures
S.5.   Increasing capabilities of adaptation

Means of obtaining information

M.1.   Surveys
M.2.   Sample surveys
M.3.   Questionnaires

VI. Identification of the learner's needs by the teaching establishment in relation to its objectives

VI.B *Before the course*

Like learners, teaching establishments very often have only a vague idea of the objectives they seek to attain through the instruction given. If they wish to adopt unit/credit systems they will need to define them precisely at two levels – general and operational so that in the first place they may offer them to future learners and discuss them with them and secondly so that they may be in a position to help the learners to fix their own objectives. Like them they must make the same effort to become aware by whom and in what manner the aims of their teaching are defined and what pressures and influences the establishments can directly or indirectly bring to bear on the learner.

Types of information

T.1.   Level of description of objectives

T.1.1.   Long-term objectives
T.1.1.1.   General objectives
T.1.1.2.   Operational objectives
T.1.2.   Short-term objectives
T.1.2.1.   General objectives
T.1.2.2.   Operational objectives

T.2.   Areas in which the language is intended to be used

T.2.1.   Private life
T.2.2.   Working life

T.3. Content of objectives

T.3.1.   Phonetics
T.3.2.   Morphology
T.3.3.   Syntax
T.3.4.   Lexis
T.3.5.   Referential objects
T.3.6.   Language activities
T.3.7.   Language functions
T.3.8.   Language situations
T.3.9.   Understanding speech
T.3.10.   Understanding written matter
T.3.11.   Speaking
T.3.12.   Writing
T.3.13.   General content (textbooks, methods, threshold level)

T.4. Who defines the objectives?

T.4.1.   The administrative section
T.4.2.   The educational section
T.4.3.   The teachers
T.4.4.   The learners
T.4.5.   The material used
T.4.6.   Through negotiation

T.5. Who supplies information about the objectives?

T.5.1.   Publicity materials
T.5.2.   The Secretariat
T.5.3.   The educational section
T.5.4.   The teacher

T.6. In what form?

T.6.1.   In prospectuses, advertisements, by demonstrations
T.6.2.   In syllabuses
T.6.3.   In pre-prepared lists (eg threshold levels)
T.6.4.   In the material used
T.6.5.   In the teaching
T.6.6.   In interviews

Possible steps to be taken by the teaching establishment

S.1.   Acceptance of objectives laid down in the material used
S.2.   Altering those objectives and producing suitable additional material
S.3.   Defining objectives and selecting appropriate material
S.4.   Discussing the objectives with learners and defining them jointly with the latter
S.5.   Discussing pre-prepared lists of objectives with the learners

Means of obtaining information

M.1.   Interviews

34

M.2.   Pre-prepared lists of objectives
M.3.   Methods of defining objectives

VI.D During the course

In learner-centred systems, specification of objectives must not take place only before the course but must continue throughout. The role of the teacher becomes vital here since it is up to him to introduce permanent procedures for defining, discussing and revising and to make sure that they are used. His task will be made easier if such procedures are an integral part of the material, failing which he will be obliged to adopt a personal method of teaching by objectives. The establishment, for its part, must have fairly adaptable organisational structures so that it may amend its own objectives in line with those of the learners.

The types of information to be collected are the same as those specified earlier under VI.B, so that we need only repeat the chapter headings.

Types of information

T.1.   *Level of description of objectives*

T.2.   *Areas in which the language is intended to be used*

T.3.   *Content of objectives*

T.4.   *Who defines the objectives?*

T.5.   *Who supplies information on the objectives?*

T.6.   *In what form?*

Possible steps to be taken by the teaching establishment

S.1.   Making definition, discussion and revision procedures an integral part of the material
S.2.   Training the teachers in the practice of teaching by objectives
S.3.   Creating adaptable institutional structures

Means of obtaining information

M.1.   Interviews
M.2.   Methods of defining objectives
M.3.   Pre-prepared lists of objectives
M.4.   Questionnaires forming an integral part of the material

VII. Identification of the learner's needs by the teaching establishment in relation to its methods of assessment

VII.B Before the course

The study *Survey of curricula and performance in modern languages 1971–72* by C V James and S Rouve clearly showed how the methods of assessment used by some establishments failed to match up either to their curricula or to their definition of learning needs, where any such existed. It cannot be too often repeated that specification and assessment go hand in hand, that they cannot be separated one from another and that teaching establishments must have the necessary means of making them an integral part of the actual teaching systems they introduced.

Before the course it will be necessary to collect information enabling the teaching establishment to be organized in line with what has been achieved, the interests and personalities of the learners and the types of certificate awarded by the establishment.

Types of information

T.1. Assessment of what has been achieved

T.1.1.   Phonetics
T.1.2.   Morphology
T.1.3.   Syntax
T.1.4.   Lexis
T.1.5.   Referential objects
T.1.6.   Language activities
T.1.7.   Language functions
T.1.8.   Language situations
T.1.9.   Understanding speech
T.1.10. Reading
T.1.11. Speaking
T.1.12. Writing
T.1.13. General content (textbooks, methods, threshold levels)

T.2. Type of assessment

T.2.1.   Objective tests
T.2.2.   Interviews
T.2.3.   Reference to background, *cf* III.B, T.1.
T.2.4.   Questionnaires
T.2.5.   Entrance examinations
T.2.6.   Entrance competitions

T.3. Assessment of the learner's identity and personality

T.3.1.   *cf* I.B, T.1. and T.2.

T.4. Assessment of interests

T.4.1.   Areas in working life
T.4.2.   Areas in private life

T.5. Grouping of learners

T.5.1.   By reference to what they have achieved
T.5.2.   By reference to interests
T.5.3.   By reference to personality
T.5.4.   By reference to identity (age, occupation)
T.5.5.   By reference to language background
T.5.6.   By reference to methods chosen (language laboratory, audio-visual methods etc)

T.5.7. By reference to resources (time, place, financial resources etc)
T.5.8. By reference to objectives
T.5.9. By reference to course chosen (size of group, profile of teacher etc)

T.6. Types of qualification

T.6.1. Official diploma
T.6.2. Non-offical diploma
T.6.3. Testimonial
T.6.4. Certificate
T.6.5. Unit/credit
T.6.6. With marks
T.6.7. Without marks
T.6.8. With comments
T.6.9. Without comments

T.7. Content of qualification

T.7.1. *cf* T.1. above

Possible steps to be taken by teaching establishment

S.1. Provide the necessary means of assessment
S.2. Organize a guidance service

Means of obtaining information

M.1. Aptitude tests
M.2. Personality tests
M.3. Attitude scales
M.4. Tests of aptitude for languages
M.5. Selection tests
M.6. Classification tests
M.7. Questionnaires
M.8. Interviews

VII.D During the course

Assessment during the course is intended firstly to enable the learner to find his feet *vis-à-vis* the instruction he is to take and secondly to enable the establishment to have a permanent check on whether the teaching systems used are suitable and whether they are functioning properly. In this connection we use the types of information specified under III.D, together with those enabling an assessment to be made of the operation of the systems as a whole.

Types of information

T.1. Conditions of assessment
    cf III.D, T.1.

T.2. Types of assessment
    cf III.D, T.2.

T.3. *Level of assessment*
cf III.D, T.3.

T.4. *Content of assessment*
cf III.D, T.4.

T.5. *Types of qualification*
cf VII. B, T.6.

T.6. *Contents of qualification*
cf VII.B, T.1.

T.7. *Who awards the qualification*

T.7.1.   The teacher
T.7.2.   A panel of teachers
T.7.2.1.   For an internal qualification
T.7.2.2.   For an external qualification
T.7.3.   Someone from outside the establishment
T.7.3.1.   For an internal qualification
T.7.3.2.   For an external qualification
T.7.4.   A panel of people from outside the teaching establishment
T.7.4.1.   For an internal qualification
T.7.4.2.   For an external qualification

T.8. *Assessment of systems*

T.8.1.   Learner's reactions to the group
T.8.2.   To the material
T.8.3.   To the surroundings
T.8.4.   To technical aids used
T.8.5.   To the teacher
T.8.6.   To the administration
T.8.7.   To the educational executives
T.8.8.   To the Secretariat
T.8.9.   To use of the language outside the teaching establishment

Possible steps to be taken by the teaching establishment

S.1.   Incorporate methods of assessment in the material used
S.2.   Selecting these at the same time as the objectives are defined
S.3.   Be capable of making quick decisions so as to make changes arising out of information obtained (alterations in the composition of groups, changes of material, teachers etc)

Means of obtaining information

M.1.   Examination tests
M.2.   Progress tests
M.3.   Self-assessment
M.4.   Questionnaires
M.5.   Observation
M.6.   Content analysis

38

VIII. Identification of the learner's needs by the teaching establishment in relation to its syllabuses

VIII.B Before the course

Obviously an establishment cannot provide every learner with a special curriculum to suit his particular needs. It must nevertheless try to offer as wide a choice as possible so that each learner can find at least some facilities suited to his expectations and requirements. Selecting a curriculum necessarily involves making a compromise. Learner-centred systems ought to operate in such a way that they enable everyone to get the best out of them.

In order to describe the curricula we would refer to much of the information given earlier, since it represents a means of attaining objectives and thus also judging whether these have been achieved as far as is possible with the resources available. It would be advisable to compile this information for each different syllabus.

Types of information

T.1. Types of establishment

    cf V.B, T.1.

T.2. Time taken up by the syllabus

T.2.1.   Number of hours a day
T.2.2.   Number of days a week
T.2.3.   Number of weeks a month
T.2.4.   Number of months a year
T.2.5.   Number of years
T.2.6.   At what time of day
T.2.7.   On which days of the week
T.2.8.   During holidays

T.3. Where learning is done

T.3.1.   In the country where the language is spoken
T.3.2.   Outside the country where the language is spoken
T.3.3.   Number of rooms needed
T.3.4.   Types of rooms needed

T.4. Cost of course

T.4.1.   Enrolment fee
T.4.2.   Cost of course
T.4.3.   Cost of materials
T.4.4.   Cost of board (with or without travelling expenses)

T.5. Teachers

T.5.1.   Number of teachers for each curriculum
T.5.2.   Teachers' qualifications

T.6. Learners

T.6.1.   Number of learners to a group
T.6.2.   Self-tuition

T.7. Technical aids to learning

T.7.1.   Language laboratory
T.7.2.   Television
T.7.3.   Radio
T.7.4.   Teaching machines
T.7.5.   Film stills
T.7.6.   Slides
T.7.7.   Films
T.7.8.   Other visual aids
T.7.9.   Recorded tapes
T.7.10   Cassettes
T.7.11. Records
T.7.12. Other auditive aids
T.7.13. Printed matter

T.8. Material used in the course

T.8.1.   Material bought on the market
T.8.2.   Original material
T.8.3.   Additional original material
T.8.4.   One-off material
T.8.5.   Material in several copies

T.9. Areas in which curriculum is used

T.9.1.   Working life
T.9.2.   Private life

T.10 Content of course
  cf VI.B, T.3.

T.11. Methods used in the course

T.11.1.   Method determined by the material
T.11.2.   Original methods
T.11.3.   Additional original activities
T.11.4   Method depending on the teacher

T.12. Levels taught

T.12.1.   Beginners
T.12.2.   False beginners
T.12.3.   Intermediate stage
T.12.4.   Advanced stage
T.12.5.   Further training stage

Possible steps to be taken by the teaching establishment

S.1.   Describing curricula in detail but so as to be understandable to a non-specialist
S.2.   Negotiating curricula with the learner in order to arrive at a compromise between his needs and the establishment's facilities for meeting them

Means of obtaining information

M.1.   Questionnaires
M.2.   Interviews

VIII.D During the course

Since the learner's needs will change during the course, the teaching establishment should be capable of adapting its syllabuses in line with changes as they are confirmed. Obviously this requires flexible organizational structures such as are in most cases incompatible with institutional rigidity. The attempt to achieve such flexibility is, however, one of the main conditions for the use of unit/credit systems of learning. Thus the teaching establishment must constantly raise certain questions regarding the different component parts of its syllabuses so that where necessary it may decide to alter some of them.

Types of information

T.1.   Types of establishment

T.1.1.   Will changes made in the syllabuses make any difference to the establishment's status and reputation?

T.2.   Time taken up by the syllabus

T.2.1.   Is it necessary to change the amount of time devoted to syllabuses?

T.3.   Where teaching is done

T.3.1.   Is it necessary to make any changes in the places where the courses are held?

T.4.   Cost of course

T.4.1.   Should the cost of courses be increased or reduced?

T.5.   Teachers

T.5.1.   Would it be advisable to make any change in the length of time teachers are employed?
T.5.2.   Do they need retraining?
T.5.3.   Do any teachers need to be recruited or dismissed?

T.6.   Learners

T.6.1.   Must the composition of groups necessarily be altered?

T.7.   Technical aids to learning

T.7.1.   Should any technical aids be purchased or disposed of?
T.7.2.   Should other uses of them be contemplated?

T.8.   Material used in the course

T.8.1.   Should further material be purchased or produced?

T.9.   Areas in which curriculum is used

T.9.1.   Is there need to specialize in any sphere?
T.9.2.   Should any areas be added or dropped?

T.10.   Contents of syllabus

T.10.1.   Is there a need for changes in the contents of the syllabus?

T.11.   Methods used in the course

T.11.1.   Is it necessary to make any change in the methods used?

T.12.   Grades taught

T.12.1.   Is it necessary to distinguish differently between the levels of syllabuses?
T.12.2.   Is it necessary to add or drop courses at certain levels?

Possible steps to be taken by the teaching establishment

S.1.   Negotiate possible desirable changes with the learners
S.2.   Introduce flexible organizational structures
S.3.   Increase capabilities of adjustment

Means of obtaining information

M.1.   Interviews
M.2.   Questionnaires
M.3.   Observation
M.4.   Content analysis

7. IDENTIFICATION OF THE LEARNER'S NEEDS BY THE USER-INSTITUTION

IX. Identification of the learner's needs by the user-institution in relation to its resources

By user-institution we mean any structurized social unit making use of one or more foreign languages to enable it to operate properly. This therefore includes both large firms or businesses and administrative bodies and small traders or families. In any given society it is they who are more or less responsible for directly or indirectly determining the needs of learners and teaching establishments. It may be found that information circulates somewhat inefficiently between the different levels and that the expression of an individual's needs is subject to all kinds of pressures and censoring from teaching bodies, users and society.

The identification of needs carried out in or by these institutions is extremely important because it is here that we can observe the real use of foreign languages, thus enabling us to secure information from which to specify objectives and syllabuses. We are here looking mainly at those user-institutions which undertake to provide language tuition for their employees either by giving them opportunities of learning at the institution's own centres or by sending them to an outside establishment. We shall make use of the same outline as previously but without the heading 'During the course' since they are not themselves directly involved in teaching; and we shall restrict the types of information because to describe these in detail would take up too much space in this study.

Types of information

T.1.   Types of institution

T.1.1.   National and local government services
T.1.2.   Private businesses

T.2.   Staff

T.2.1.   Number employed
T.2.2.   In administration
T.2.3.   In technical work
T.2.4.   In manufacture
T.2.5.   In training duties
T.2.6.   In personnel section
T.2.7.   Management
T.2.8.   Executives
T.2.9.   Clerical workers
T.2.10.   Manual workers
T.2.11.   Labourers

T.3.   Length of time employed

T.3.1.   Full-time staff
T.3.2.   Part-time staff

T.3.3.   People employed for a particular job
T.3.4.   Hours of work
T.3.5.   Time devoted to training
T.3.6.   Study leave

T.4.   Place and location

T.4.1.   Number of establishments
T.4.2.   Type of building
T.4.3.   Type of premises
T.4.4.   Country
T.4.5.   Region
T.4.6.   Small place
T.4.7.   Average-sized town
T.4.8.   Large town
T.4.9.   City suburbs
T.4.10. City centre

T.5.   Financial arrangements

T.5.1.   General budget
T.5.2.   Budgets for different sections
T.5.3.   Wages and salaries of various classes of employee

Possible steps to be taken by the user-institution

S.1.   User-institutions usually keep this kind of information up to date
S.2.   In order to obtain fuller information they may also consult an organization specializing in institutional analysis

Means of obtaining information

M.1.   Statistics
M.2.   Questionnaires

X. Identification of the learner's needs by the user-institution in relation to its objectives

At user-institution level the identification of needs in relation to objectives will consist mainly in describing what the people living and working there do with the language or languages used.

From this description they can proceed to define the objectives and curricula best suited to requirements

Types of information

T.1.   Level of description of objectives

T.1.1.   General objectives
T.1.2.   Operational objectives

T.2. Areas in which used

T.2.1. At work
T.2.2. In private life

T.3. Content of objectives

T.3.1. Language activities
T.3.2. Language functions
T.3.3. Language situations
T.3.4. Referential objects

T.4. Language skills practised

T.4.1. Understanding speech
T.4.2. Understanding writing
T.4.3. Speaking
T.4.4. Writing

T.5. Frequency with which languages are used

T.5.1. Frequently
T.5.2. Occasionally
T.5.3. Rarely

T.6. Who defines the objectives

T.6.1. The user
T.6.2. The personnel department
T.6.3. An internal teaching establishment
T.6.4. An external teaching establishment
T.6.5. A body specializing in institutional analysis
T.6.6. An internal observer
T.6.7. An external observer
T.6.8. By negotiation (trade unions, employers' associations, works councils)

Possible steps to be taken by the user-institution

S.1. Making an analysis of its own means
S.2. Consulting a body specializing in institutional analysis
S.3. Consulting a teaching establishment

Means of obtaining information

M.1. Questionnaires
M.2. Interviews
M.3. Observation
M.4. Job analysis
M.5. Content analysis

XI. Identification of the learner's needs by the user-institution in relation to its methods of assessment

It is essential that the individual should know how his abilities are going to be assessed by the user-institution and that the latter should clearly understand – which is not always the case – the criteria adopted by it for such assessment, the results of which may have a decisive influence on the behaviour, motivations and attitudes of the users. The latter should be able to share in their own assessment.

Types of information

T.1. Assessment on enrolment

T.1.1. Tests of aptitude for the language or languages
T.1.2. Selection tests
T.1.3. Classification tests
T.1.4. Personality tests
T.1.5. Psychological aptitude tests
T.1.6. Interviews
T.1.7. Competitive tests
T.1.8. Examinations

T.2. Types of qualification demanded

T.2.1. University degree
T.2.2. Professional or vocational qualification
T.2.3. School-leaving certificate giving access to a university
T.2.4. Diploma, testimonial or certificate issued by a private school
T.2.5. Diploma, testimonial or certificate issued by an official or semi-official permanent education establishment
T.2.6. References
T.2.7. Recommendations
T.2.8. Certificate issued by another user-institution

T.3. Continuous assessment

T.3.1. Observation and supervision at place where language is used
T.3.2. Periodical interviews
T.3.3. Periodical examinations
T.3.4. Competitive tests leading to promotion
T.3.5. Objective tests given periodically

T.4. Result of assessment

T.4.1. Promotion to a higher job
T.4.2. Social promotion
T.4.3. Increase in salary
T.4.4. Increased responsibility
T.4.5. Wider choice of jobs
T.4.6. More varied tasks
T.4.7. Opportunity for training
T.4.8. Dismissal

T.5.1.   A colleague
T.5.2.   A superior
T.5.3.   The personnel department
T.5.4.   The management
T.5.5.   An outsider observer
T.5.6.   The user himself
T.5.7.   A teaching establishment
T.5.8.   A group of colleagues
T.5.9.   A mixed group (eg 5.1. + 5.2. + 5.5.)

Possible steps to be taken by the user-institutions

S.1.   Laying down coherent criteria for engaging, assessing and promoting
S.2.   Arranging for the user to have a share in his own assessment

Means of obtaining information

M.1.   Observation
M.2.   Interviews
M.3.   Different kinds of psychological tests
M.4.   Different kinds of language tests

XII. Identification of the learner's needs by the user-institution in relation to its programmes

In the case of user-institutions the term 'programme' must be understood to mean the methods, opportunities and facilities which they offer to individuals for learning one or more foreign languages. The institutions themselves will not give training as such, except by the use which they make of the language or languages in their work, and they will have to turn to either an internal teaching centre or an outside establishment in order to negotiate jointly with them and the future learner the syllabuses as these have been described under VIII.B.

Types of information

T.1.   Time spent on training

T.1.1.   Courses taken partly during working time
T.1.2.   Courses taken entirely during working time (continuous or non-continuous study leave)
T.1.3.   Courses taken entirely outside working hours
T.1.4.   Length of course

T.2.   Place where courses are taken

T.2.1.   At an internal teaching centre
T.2.2.   At an external teaching establishment
T.2.3.   At the place of work
T.2.4.   At home

T.3.   *Payment for training*

T.3.1.   Paid by the institution
T.3.2.   Paid by the public authorities
T.3.3.   Full payment provided
T.3.4.   Part payment provided
T.3.5.   Study leave on full pay
T.3.6.   Study leave on part pay
T.3.7.   Unpaid study leave

T.4.   *Learners*

T.4.1.   Number of persons whose courses are partially paid for
T.4.2.   Number of persons whose courses are fully paid for

T.5.   *Syllabuses*

    cf. VIII.B, 1 to 12

Possible steps to be taken by the user-institution

S.1.   Inform individuals of their entitlement to training and the facilities available
S.2.   User-institution's training programmes
S.3.   Negotiate courses with the centre or the teaching establishment
S.4.   Negotiate training programmes with the future learners

Means of obtaining information

M.1.   Interviews
M.2.   Questionnaires

APPENDIX I: IDENTIFYING LANGUAGE NEEDS IN FOUR DIFFERENT CASES

Types of information to be obtained for Case 1:

A person who wants to learn English, enrolls at a teaching establishment and studies there

(The numbers and letters refer to those in the section 'Types of information')

Before the course				During the course			
	Essential	Advisable			Essential	Advisable	
I B	T1, T3, T4, T5	T2		I D	T3, T4, T5	T1, T2	
II B	T1, T3	T2, T4		II D	T3, T4	T1, T2	
III B	T1, T2, T3	T4		III D	T2, T4	T1, T3	
IV B	T1, T2, T3, T4, T9, T11	T5, T6, T7, T8 T10, T12, T13		IV D	T1, T2, T3, T4, T9, T11	T5, T6, T7, T8, T10, T12, T13	

Types of information to be obtained for Case 2:

A person who wants to learn German and is learning it by self-tuition merely for pleasure

Before the course				During the course			
	Essential	Advisable			Essential	Advisable	
I B	T1, T5	T2, T3		I D	T2, T3, T5	T1, T4	
II B	T3	T1, T2, T4		II D	T4	T1, T2, T3	
III B	T1	T2, T3, T4		III D		T1, T2, T3, T4	
IV B	T4	T2, T7, T9, T10, T11, T12, T13		IV D	T4	T2, T7, T8, T9, T10, T11, T12	

Types of information to be obtained for Case 3:

A teaching establishment that wants to organize and adapt its methods of teaching French to fit in with the demand

Before the course				During the course			
	Essential	Advisable			Essential	Advisable	
I B	T1, T3, T4, T5	T2		I D	T2, T3, T4, T5	T1	
II B	T1, T3, T4	T2		II D	T1, T3	T2, T4	
III B	T1, T2, T3	T4		III D	T2, T3, T4	T1	
IV B	T2, T3, T4, T6 T9, T10, T11	T5, T7, T8, T12, T13		IV D	T2, T3, T4, T5, T6, T7, T8, T9, T10, T11, T12, T13	T1	
V B	T1, T4, T7	T2, T3, T5, T6		V D	T3, T4, T5, T6	T1, T2	
VI B	T1, T3	T2, T4, T5, T6		VI D	T1, T3	T2, T4, T5, T6	
VII B	T1, T2, T5, T6, T7	T3, T4		VII D	T1, T2, T3, T4, T5, T6, T7, T8		
VIII B	T1, T2, T4, T5 T6, T7, T8, T10, T11, T12	T3, T9		VIII D	T1, T2, T3, T4 T5, T6, T7, T8, T9, T10, T11, T12		
IX B							
X	T3	T1, T2, T4, T5, T6					
XI	T1, T2	T3, T4, T5					
XII		T1, T3, T5					

Types of information to be obtained for Case 4:

A user-institution that has decided to give its commercial executives a knowledge of Spanish to enable them to canvass South-American markets

		Essential			Advisable
I	B	T1, T3, T4, T5	I	B	T2
II	B		II	B	T1, T2, T3, T4
III	B	T1, T2, T3, T4			
IV	B	T1, T2, T3, T4, T11	IV	B	T5, T6, T7, T8, T9, T10, T12, T13
V	B		V	B	T1, T2, T4, T5, T7
VI	B		VI	B	T1, T2, T3, T4, T5, T6
VII	B	T6	VII	B	T1, T2, T4, T5, T7
VIII	B		VIII	B	T1, T2, T3, T4, T5, T6, T7, T8, T9, T10, T11, T12
IX		T1, T2, T3, T4, T5			
X		T1, T2, T3, T4, T5, T6			
XI		T1, T2, T3, T4, T5			
XII		T1, T2, T3, T4, T5			

PART THREE:
METHODS OF COLLECTION

8. INTRODUCTION

General

For any identification of needs it is first of all necessary to collect data. For every fact or experience a certain amount of information exists which is held by one or more persons, which may be found in several printed sources in one or more places, and which may be accessible by means of one or more methods of research. Let us take, for example, the case of a commercial executive who has to learn a language in order to go out selling products in a foreign country. In the first place the data has to be collected from him in order to find out how much he is prepared to invest in learning, what are his attitudes towards the language, what previous knowledge he has and so on. But it will also be in the hands of other people already engaged in this type of activity, who will be able to say what abilities are needed, and of the head of the personnel section who can give information on what the job entails, what responsibilities it involves etc. To collect this different data it will be necessary to use various methods and to contact different people. Between existing data and the data used for the purpose of organizing teaching systems there are a number of channels in passing through which it is in danger of becoming distorted and parasitical. We can distinguish between the following levels:

Figure 2

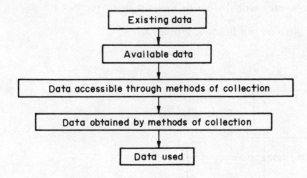

It is interesting to consider how data passes from one stratum to another:

Existing data becomes available data

Here we recognize censoring phenomena which may be of a psychological or sociological nature. This is the whole problem of the existence and nature of channels of communication which either censor the whole or part of the data or else are entirely non-existent.

Available data becomes data accessible through methods of collection

Not all available data is necessarily accessible to methods of collection. This may be either because it is fixed by those methods (this is the case with methods aimed at changing data that is available in oral form into data available in written form, ie, from being non-fixed it becomes fixed) or because the method of collection used changes the essential nature of the data (eg in non-directive interviews which presuppose progressive realization by the person concerned of data which he or she has about his or her own situation).

Accessible data becomes data obtained by the methods of collection

The methods of collection are more or less structuring. They take from the data available only what they derive from experience. We can make a comparison with the sensory organs. If we stand in front of a landscape we can stop up our ears so that the only impressions we get come from sight or smell; if we close our eyes there is nothing left but smells. From the countryside as it exists we have extracted data depending on the sensory organ or organs that have remained functional . The same thing applies to methods of collection, which are simply channels of communication introduced for the purpose of causing the information to emerge so that it can be made use of. As a result, they make it figurable: a questionnaire can explore only what the questions explore; in the same way, we have little control over the level of expression in non-directive interviews.

Data obtained becomes data used

Not all the data obtained will be used, either because it will not be thought relevant to the problem to be solved or because the methods of processing the data (content analysis, statistics, etc) will distort or censor all or part of it.

We can sum this up in the following diagram:

Figure 3

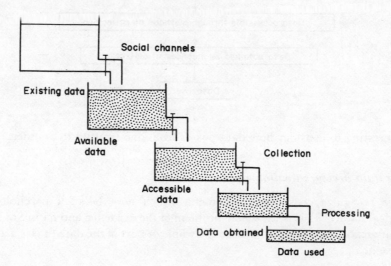

We can distinguish two main kinds of method:

– those whose aim is essentially to collect all the necessary data from that available depending on objectives (interviews, questionnaires, job analyses, etc);
– those which attempt to process this information in such a way as to render it usable for the purpose of achieving the objectives (statistics, content analysis, etc)

9. SURVEYS

1. Definition

A survey is the construction, introduction and use of methods of collecting and processing data with the object of arriving at the fullest and most authentic description of a field of study. Based on the results of the survey it is possible to plan action aimed at bringing about some change or adaptation.

2. Principles and classification

A system of teaching is defined by means of organizational structures, institutional and educational objectives and resources. In order to define all these aspects it is necessary to collect a certain amount of data. This latter may relate to the existing situation (descriptive survey), production relationships, the needs of a population (micro-census), statistical data relating to a population (age, sex, activity, socio-cultural level, previous training etc), attitude towards teaching, languages, learning of languages, and collective representations. In earlier pages we have given details of the types of data to be collected. Each of these may be the subject of a survey.

We can distinguish three kinds:

2.1. The pin-pointing survey

This is intended to evaluate the situation of a population in relation to one variable or a group of variables at any given time (eg a compilation of data on the attitudes of future learners towards an audio-visual method).

2.2. The research/action type of survey

This is more clinical in inspiration and is merely an analyzer enabling a population to understand the nature of its needs and resources.

2.3. Research/evaluation

This is a combination of the first two categories and is an analyzer enabling assessments to be made and action taken.

3. Principles of construction

A survey may be split up into three phases:

3.1. The preliminary survey

The object of this is to determine the hypotheses, define the population and construct the means of collecting data. The following five stages may be distinguished:

- recording data already known;
- ascertaining unknown data;
- grading and processing data by content analysis
  methods (see that expression);

- defining the hypotheses.   Defining the population to
                               which the collection of data is
                               to be applied;

- constructing the means of collecting data for the survey.

At the end of the preliminary survey we should have defined the hypotheses, the population and the means of collecting data.

3.2. Testing

This phase consists of validating the means of collecting data.

3.3. The survey

This is made up of four phases:

- collection of data;
- processing this data:
  - tabulating the data,
  - content analysis and statistical analysis;
- presenting the results,
- converting the results into action.

4. Application*

A survey may enable us to determine the amount of time which learners can devote to their studies. The results will help teaching establishments to draw up their syllabuses more efficiently and adjust them to the different classes of learner. It may also enable two or more types of variable to be brought into relationship, eg types of use of a second language with instructional material and educational techniques desired by the future learners. This will make it possible to make up groups centred on use and the desired educational methods.

---

* cf– Billiez, J, et al (1975) *Étude de la demande de formation en langue étrangère de la population adulte de l'agglomération grenobloise.*
   – Emmans, K, E Hawkins and A Westoby (1974) *Foreign languages in industry/commerce.*
   – Österreichisches Statistisches Zentralamt (1976) *Fremdsprachenkenntnisse der österreichischen Bevölkerung.*

10. SAMPLE SURVEYS

1. Definition

A sample survey is a method of estimating certain characteristics of a population by means of a suitably selected sample.

2. Principles and classification

We start with a given population which is a body of people having at least one common characteristic. By the presence or absence of that characteristic it is thus possible to determine whether a person belongs to a population or not. All individuals sharing the same characteristic make up the *basis of sampling* from which a *sample* is drawn, this being a sub-unit from which certain parameters of that population can be estimated. Estimating means that there is some danger of inexactitude.

A parameter is measured by reference to a sample (t).

For the total population the parameter has the value (T).

$E = T - t$ is called the *sampling error*.

In this total sampling error we can distinguish three components:

- the *sampling error* due to the fact that the measurement has been taken on a sample and not on the whole population;
- *biases* resulting from the collection of data;
- the *random error of measurement* due to coding, recording and processing this data.

Sample survey techniques

There are two methods:

- *Sample surveys based on probabilities:* These are used wherever the basis of sampling can be exhaustively defined. The methods used are:

- selection at random;
- selection from random number tables;
- systematic selection. If the sample is to be one in fifteen, every fifteenth person is taken from a list of people starting from a number between one and fifteen chosen at random;
- multi-stage random sampling: a population is divided up into a number of groups. From each of these a selection is made either at random or on a systematic basis. These groups can be defined on the basis of a control variable.

- *Sample surveys not based on probabilities:* These are used when there is no basis of sampling.

- *the standard unit method:* A person possesses a certain number of characteristics. It is assumed that if such a person represents the average in respect of one characteristic (eg income) it is highly probable that he will also be in an average situation as regards others (money available for learning a language, amount of time at his disposal, and so on). The average is therefore calculated for a certain number of characteristics (income) and the matters inquired about are defined in terms of their proximity to this latter;

- *quota method:* It is assumed that in any population characteristics are not independent one of the other (socio-economic status and income, for example). Thus if we know some of them we can carry out a sample survey. However, it is essential that these variables (termed control variables) should be known and that they should be easily identifiable in the field. *This is the method which is the most easy to use for needs surveys.*

3. Principles of construction: included with 2.

4. Application*

If it is desired to draw up language-teaching syllabuses for a population living in a given area it is not possible to make a full list of all the people concerned. It is therefore necessary to use the method of estimating, ie to make a survey of a sample and find out what languages the people wish to learn or the reasons why they are learning one at present.

A country may wish to know what the requirements of its citizens are in the matter of learning languages. It is difficult to question all of them. A sample survey based on probabilities will therefore be conducted on the basis of a list of all the inhabitants.

---

* *cf* Österreichisches Statistisches Zentralamt (1976) *Fremdsprachenkenntnisse der österreichischen Bevölkerung.*

11. QUESTIONNAIRES

1. Definition

Questionnaires are structured instruments for the collection of data which translate research hypotheses into questions.

2. Principles and classification

Questionnaires may be said to have two functions:
- the question must induce the person questioned to express an opinion or state a fact which it is important to know;
- the question must be related to the person's circumstances so that he or she shall give the information in his or her possession as precisely as possible.

There are three methods of communication:
- *the personal interview*
- *inquiry by mail*
- *inquiry by telephone*

Four types of questionnaires are found:
- *Questionnaires consisting of closed questions.* The person questioned selects the answers from a number of possibilities offered.

Example: What is your marital status?

Unmarried	☐
Married	☐
Widower	☐
Divorced	☐

No other answers are possible. From the answers to two questions it is possible to construct cross-tables:

Figure 4

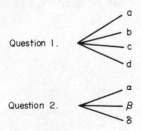

	a	b	c	d
a	aa	ab	ac	ad
β	βa	βb	βc	βd
δ	δa	δb	δc	δd

It is very difficult for closed questions to elicit slight differences. The answer is conditioned by the framework of the questions put.

- *Questionnaires consisting of open questions.* These do not call in advance for ready-made answers and therefore allow the person questioned more freedom of expression. However, what is gained in freedom is lost in validity and accuracy.

– *Mixed questionnaires.* Using both kinds of questions (closed and open).

– *Graded questionnaires.* These are questionnaires in which, thanks to the use of suitable questions, it is possible to classify the individual members of a population into graded groups (positive or negative attitudes).

Figure 5

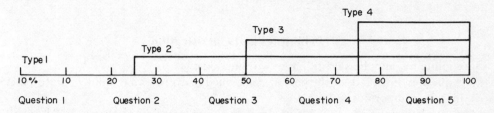

Questions 1 and 5 are limit questions and relate to extreme attitudes (positive or negative). The others (2, 3, 4) divide the population into two sub-groups. In this way it is possible to distinguish four groups of people according to the presence (1) or the absence (0) of a characteristic:

Figure 6

Type 1	0 1 1 1 1
Type 2	0 0 1 1 1
Type 3	0 0 0 1 1
Type 4	0 0 0 0 1

These graded questionnaires enable us to construct typologies of people, educational materials etc.

3. Principles of construction

Before we can construct any questionnaire it is necessary to conduct a preliminary survey which will supply us with three types of data:

– hypotheses;
– a knowledge of the population:
    – category to which people belong
    – communication networks
    – method of expression
    – level of expression;
– objectives of the investigation.

Based on these latter we can distinguish three stages:

– macrostructuring in which each objective is taken up and analyzed into sub-objectives until we reach a balance between hypotheses and sub-objectives. We then have a tree-like structure with comparable hypothesis levels;

60

- mesostructuring which is the conversion of each sub-objective into questions;
- microstructuring which relates to the elements of the question itself.

4. Application*

A questionnaire may be used for any objective collection of data. However, the manner in which the question is put influences the answer. Questionnaires are useful in all cases where data regarding a population is more important than information about particular individuals. Thus for example a questionnaire will enable us to describe and classify the reasons why people wish to take a given course of instruction. It may help us to get to know the teaching methods which a group would like to see applied when learning a language.

(See example below in *Appendices II, III* and *IV*.)

* cf– Österreichisches Statistisches Zentralamt (1976) *Fremdsprachenkenntnisse der österreichischen Bevölkerung*
   – Billiez, J, et al, (1975) *Étude de la demande de formation en langue étrangère de la population adulte de l'agglomération grenobloise*
   – Emmans, K, E Hawkins and A Westoby (1974) *Foreign languages in industry/commerce*. Pilot survey of national manpower requirements in foreign languages.

APPENDIX II: FREMDSPRACHENKENTNISSE DER ÖSTERREICHISCHEN BEVÖLKERUNG PERSONENBLATT

Österreichisches Statistisches Zentralamt

MIKROZENSUS

1974-4/DEZEMBER

0123456789

Personenblatt B

① Familienname ——— Vorname

② Auskunft: Selbst erteilt — Andere Person —

③ Evidenz: Geburt — Tod — Zuzug — Wegzug — Haushaltswechsel —

④ Alter

⑤ Stellung zum Haushaltsvorstand: HV — Ehegatte des HV — Kind des HV — Eltern (Schwiegerelt.) des HV — Verwandter Verschw. des HV — Fam.-fremde Person —

⑥ Geschlecht: Männl. — Weiblich —

⑦ Österreicher: Ja — Nein —

Kennzahlen Bezirk Inter-viewer

⑧ Familienstand: Ledig — Verheiratet — Ver-witwet — Geschieden —

⑨ Teilnahme am Erwerbsleben: Beschäftigt — Arbeitslos (Lehrstelle suchend) — Pensionist, Rentner — Nicht berufstätige Hausfrau — Student, Schüler — Vorschulpfl. Kind — Sonstige erhaltene Person —

⑩ Berufliche Tätigkeit

⑪ Betriebszweig

Wohnung Haushalt Person

⑫ Stellung im Beruf: Selbständiger — Angestellter — Mithelfend Fam.-Angeh. — Arbeiter — Beamter — Lehrling/Arbeiterberuf — Lehrling/Angest.-Beruf —

⑬ Normale wöchentliche Arbeitszeit — Stunden

⑭ Tatsächliche Arbeitszeit in der letzten Woche: Normal — Länger — Kürzer oder keine —

⑮ — Stunden

⑯ Hier keine Eintragungen! 10. 11.

Fragebogentext 1952 (An alle im Mikrozensus erfassten Personen von 15 bis 70 Jahren.)

17) Auskunft abgelehnt: —

18) Fremdsprache gelernt? Ja — Nein —

19) Welche Fremdsprache? Englisch — Französisch — / Spanisch — Italienisch — / Russisch — Andere Sprache —

20) Deutsch als Fremdsprache gelernt? Ja — Nein —

21) Fremdsprache mit den besten (zweitbesten) Kenntnissen erlernt: Beste — Zweitbeste — / Englisch — Französisch — Spanisch — Italienisch — Russisch — Andere Sprache —

22) Fremdsprache mit den besten Kenntnissen erlernt: In Österreich — / In einem Land mit dieser Sprache — / Sonstiges Land — / Nur in d. Schule — Außerhalb d. Schule — Sowohl als auch —

23) Fremdsprache gelernt: Nur in d. Schule — Außerhalb d. Schule — Sowohl als auch —

24) Fremdsprache überwiegend erlernt durch: Selbststudium — Sprachschule — Radio-, Fernsehkurs — Anderen Sprachkurs — Auf andere Weise —

25) Zeitaufwand für Sprachstudium: Bis $\frac{1}{2}$ Jahr — 1-2 Jahre — Mehr als 2 Jahre —

26) Anwendung der Fremdsprachenkenntnisse: Regelmässig — Gelegentlich — Nie —

27) Anwendungsmöglichkeit: Verstehen — Sprechen — Schreiben — Lesen — / Sehr wichtig / Wichtig / Weniger wichtig / Unwichtig

28) Fremdsprache mit den zweitbesten Kenntnissen / 2. Fremdsprache erlernt: In Österreich — / In einem Land mit dieser Sprache — / Sonstiges Land —

29) 2. Fremdsprache gelernt: Nur in d. Schule — Außerhalb d. Schule — Sowohl als auch —

30) 2. Fremdsprache überwiegend erlernt durch: Selbststudium — Sprachschule — Radio-, Fernsehkurs — Anderen Sprachkurs — Auf andre Weise —

31) Zeitaufwand für 2. Sprachstudium: Bis $\frac{1}{2}$ Jahr — 1-2 Jahre — Mehr als 2 Jahre —

Gegenwärtiges Sprachstudium (an alle von 15-70!)

32) Wird eine Fremdsprache gelernt? Ja — Nein —

33) Welche Fremdsprache? Englisch — Französisch — / Spanisch — Italienisch — / Russisch — Andere Sprache —

34) Fremdsprache wird überwiegend gelernt durch: Selbststudium — Sprachschule — Radio-, Fernsehkurs — Anderen Sprachkurs — Auf andere Weise —

Abbruch eines Sprachstudiums (an alle von 15-70!)

35) Sprachstudium einmal aufgegeben? Ja — Nein —

Beabsichtigtes Sprachstudium (an alle von 15-70!)

36) Abgeschlossene Schulen: Volksschule — Hauptschule — Allgemeinbildende höhere Schule — Berufsbildende mittlere Schule — Berufsbildende höhere Schule — Hochschule —

37) Lernabsicht im nächsten Jahr: Ja — Nein —

38) Welche Fremdsprache? Verstehen — Sprechen — Schreiben — Lesen / Englisch — Französisch — Spanisch — Italienisch — Russisch — Tschechisch — Serbokroatisch —

39) Verwendungszweck: Beruf — Urlaub — Sonstige Anlässe —

APPENDIX III: ÉTUDE DE LA DEMANDE DE FORMATION EN LANGUE ÉTRANGÈRE DE LA POPULATION ADULTE DE L'AGGLOMÉRATION GRENOBLOISE

(Billiez, J, *et al* (1975) Vol 2, Annexes pp 26–36. *Questionnaire* Avril, 1975)

–1– En plus de votre activité principale, qu'est-ce que vous avez comme autres activités? |_|_|

–2– (S'il y a lieu) Dans cette (ou ces) activités(s) est-ce que vous avez des responsabilités?
    oui (....)
    non (....) |_|

–3– Est-ce que vous vous souvenez de publicités sur les langues ètrangères? |_|
    oui (....)
    non (....) (→ passez) la question 7
    NSP (....) (→ passez) la question 7

–4– (si oui) lesquelles? |_|_|_|

–5– Qu'est-ce qu'elles disaient? |_|_|

–6– Qu'en pensez-vous? |_|

–7– Avez-vous appris des langues étrangères au cours de votre scolarité?

oui (....)

non (....) (→ passez à la question 9)

(→ passez à la question 9)

|_|

–8– (Si oui) lesquelles?

|_|_|_|_|

–9– Pour apprendre une langue étrangère, pensez-vous qu'il soit préférable d'avoir un professeur

– français d'origine (....)

– de langue maternelle? (....)

|_|

–10– A votre avis, pour apprendre une langue étrangère, que faut-il étudier plus particulièrement? (une seule réponse possible)

– la grammaire (....)

– le vocabulaire (....)

– la prononciation (....)

– ou autre chose (....)

|_|

–11– Dans la mesure où tout vous serait possible, quelle serait d'après-vous, la meilleure formule pour apprendre une langue étrangère?

|_|_|

–12– Dans ces conditions, en combien de temps pourrait-on l'apprendre?

|_|

–13– A votre avis, qu'est-ce qui est le plus indispensable pour apprendre une langue étrangère?

– le niveau culturel (....)

– la maîtrise de soi (....)

– l'intelligence (....)

– la connaissance du pays (....)

– l'envie d'apprendre (....)

– la mémoire (....)

– avoir de l'oreille (....)

– s'exprimer facilement (....)

– le goût des contacts humains (....)

– la nécessité d'apprendre (....)

– savoir écouter (....)

– la volonté (....)

– comprendre les autres (....)

– l'ardeur au travail (....)

– ne pas être timide (....)

|_|_|

–14– A votre avis, qu'est-ce qui est le plus nécessaire dans l'apprentissage d'une langue?

– comprendre	(....)
– parler	(....)
– écrire	(....)
– lire	(....)

'_'

–15– Qu'est-ce ça évoque pour vous la langue
- allemande
- chinoise
- espagnole
- américaine
- portugaise
- russe
- italienne
- arabe
- anglaise

'_'
'_'
'_'
'_'
'_'
'_'
'_'
'_'
'_'

–16– Y-a-t-il une langue que vous ne voudriez pas apprendre?
oui (....)   laquelle?
non (....)

'_'_'

–17– Pourquoi?

'_'

–18– On entend dire souvent que les étrangers sont plus doués que les français pour apprendre les langues étrangères. qu'en pensez-vous?

'_'

–19– Est-ce que vous pensez que les méthodes traditionnelles pour apprendre une langue en France sont:

très bonnes	bonnes	moyennes	mauvaises	très mauvaises?
(....)	(....)	(....)	(....)	(....)

'_'

–20– Est-ce que vous avez eu l'occasion d'aller à l'étranger?
oui (....)
non (....) (→ Passez à la question 23)

'_'

–21– Dans quels pays?   (mettre les 6 premiers pays)

'_'_'_'_'_'_'

–22– Est-ce que c'était pour
       – voyage d'affaires, congrès   (....)
       – des vacances   (....)
       – apprendre la langue   (....)
       – autres   (....)

'_'_'_' '_'

–23– Est-ce que vous pouvez me dire quelques mots ou quelques phrases dans une langue étrangère? (demander la traduction)

'_'

–24– En dehors de votre scolarité, est-ce que vous avez essayé d'apprendre une langue étrangère?
         oui (....)
         non (....)   (→ passez à la question 43)

'_'

–25– Laquelle ou lesquelles?

'_'_'_'_'

–26– Pourquoi avez-vous choisi d'apprendre cette (ou ces) langue(s)?

–27– Comment? dans les pays tt seul avec méthode tt seul par corresp. cours part. cours de groupe	Q. 28 laquelle nom de l'organisme	Q. 29 Changt. 1 Abandon 2	Q. 30 POURQUOI?

67

–31– Pourquoi avez-vous choisi ce mode d'apprentissage? |_|

–32– Combien de temps en moyenne cela vous prend-il par semaine,
cours compris?

–33– En général, quel jour de la semaine?

–34– Et à quel moment de la journée en général? |_|

–35– A quel niveau en êtes-vous? |_|

–36– Dans cette échelle, où vous situez-vous? |_|
débutant   (....)   faux-débutant   (....)   moyen-faible   (....)
moyen-fort   (....)   perfectionnement   (....)   spécialisé   (....)

–37– Est-ce que vous avez chez vous |_|_|_|
     – une grammaire (de la langue que vous étudiez)   (....)
     – un dictionnaire (de la langue que vous étudiez)   (....)
     – un livre de cours   (....)
     – des disques, des cassettes de cours   (....)
     – des livres en langue étrangère?   (....)

–38– Est-ce que vous complétez l'enseignement que vous suivez par autre chose? |_|
          oui (....)
          non (....)

–39– Dans un avenir proche, est-ce que vous envisagez d'aller dans le pays dont vous |_|
     étudiez la langue?
          oui (....)
          non (....)
          NSP (....)

68

–40– Dans votre travail, est-ce que vous utilisez ou allez utiliser la langue que voùs apprenez?

        oui (....)

        non (....)   (→ passez à la question 45)

        NSP (....)   (→ passez à la question 45)

|'__'|

–41– Dans quelles occasions?

|'__'|

–42– Est-ce que c'est

       – quotidien   (....)

       – occasionnellement   (....)

       – souvent   (....)

       – périodiquement   (....)

       – rarement   (....)

                         (Passez à la question 45)

|'__'|

–43– Est-ce que vous aimeriez savoir une langue?

        oui (....)   laquelle?

        non (....)

|'__'__'|

–44– Pourquoi?

|'__'__'|

–45– Avez-vous déjà suivi des stages de formation ou de recyclage?

        oui (....)   lesquels?

        non (....)

|'__'|

–46– Est-ce que vous iriez à l'université pour y suivre une formation qu'elle dispense?

          oui (....)

          non (....)

          NSP (....)

|'__'|

–47– Pourquoi?

|'__'__'__'|

–48– Connaissez-vous la loi de 1971 sur la Formation Permanente?

        oui (....)   qu'est-ce-que c'est

        non (....)

        si "rien du tout" passez à la question 50

|'__'|

–49– Votre formation est-elle prise en charge?   '__'

IDENTITE

NOM   PRENOM

ADRESSE

–50– Sexe: F. (....)   M. (....)   '__'

–51– Age: – de 15 ans à 24 ans (....)   '__'
                   – de 25   à 34   (....)
                   – de 35   à 44   (....)
                   – de 45   à 54   (....)
                   – de 55   à 64   (....)
                   – de 64 et +   (....)

–52– Etes-vous
     marié(e) (....) célibataire (....) veuf(ve) (....) divorcé(e) (....)?   '__'

–53– Quelles langues étrangères parle votre conjoint?   '__'__'__'__'

–54– Est-ce qu'il en apprend une et laquelle?   '__'__'

–55– Quelle est votre langue maternelle?   '__'

–56– Quelle est la langue maternelle de votre conjoint?   '__'

–57– Quelle est la langue maternelle de vos parents?   '__'__'

−58− Avez-vous des enfants en âge scolaire?
        oui (....)
        non (....)
                                  '__'

−59− (si oui) Dans quelles classes sont-ils?   '__'__'__'__'__'

−60− Quelles langues étudient-ils?   '__'__'__'__'__'__'

−61− Quel est votre niveau scolaire?   '__'
       − primaire   (....)
       − secondaire   (....)
       − Bac   (....)
       − Supérieur   (....)

−62− Quels sont les diplômes que vous avez obtenus?   '__'
       − CEP, BEPC, BAC, Licence, etc   (....)
       − professionnel (CAP, etc)   (....)
       − pas de diplôme   (....)

−63− Quelle est votre profession?   '__'
       − entreprise
       − service

−64− Quelle est la profession de votre conjoint?   '__'

APPENDIX IV: QUESTIONNAIRE TO GRADUATES

(from Emmans, K, E Hawkins and A Westoby (1974) *Foreign languages in industry/commerce*. Pilot survey of national manpower requirements in foreign languages)

QUESTIONS 1 TO 6 ASK FOR SOME BRIEF DETAILS ABOUT YOURSELF

Q.1 In which year were you born? `19`

Q.2 Please state whether male of female? (Please tick)   Male ☐   Female ☐

Q.3 Is your mother tongue English? (Please tick)   Yes ☐   No ☐

Q.4 If No, what is your mother tongue?

Q.5 Are you in full-time employment **at the moment?** (Please tick)   Yes ☐   No ☐

Q.6 If Yes, please give below brief details of your present post:

Employer's business or industry: (eg Engineering firm; local education authority)	
Title of post: (eg Sales manager; Deputy head of comprehensive school)	
Please indicate your function in the job: (eg Negotiating sales in UK and W Europe; Administration plus some teaching 'A' level French and German)	

THIS QUESTION IS ABOUT ANY LANGUAGES YOU HAVE ACQUIRED WITHOUT INSTRUCTION:
(eg by living abroad, or because you were brought up in a home where a foreign language was spoken)

Q.7 If you have learnt any languages in this way, please give brief details below:

Language				
At what age did you start learning the language?				
How did you come to learn it? (eg living in France; my mother is Polish; my wife/husband is German)				

QUESTIONS 8 TO 14 ABOUT THE LANGUAGES YOU STUDIED WITHIN THE FULL-TIME EDUCATIONAL SYSTEM AT SCHOOL, COLLEGE, UNIVERSITY, ETC

Q.8 Please give details below of the modern language subjects you have **passed** at GCE 'O' level or equivalent: (Please include here School Certificate, Matriculation, Scottish Lower Certificate or equivalent overseas examinations).

Year passed	Language	Name of examination	Result obtained (Grade if known)

Q.9 Please give below details of the modern language subjects you have **taken** at GCE 'A' level or equivalent at any time: (Note: if you took the examination more than once, please give year of the latest occasion on which you took it). Please include here Higher School Certificate and Scottish Higher Certificate or equivalent overseas examinations.

Year taken	Language	Name of examination	Result obtained (Grade if known)

Q.10 Please give details of your first modern language degree:

Year in which you graduated:

University

Title: (eg BA Hons, BA Ord, BA Joint Hons)

Languages studied: Please state whether main, subsidiary or joint, etc)

Please give Class obtained:

Q.11 If you have embarked on a course of study for **any other degree(s)** involving foreign languages, please give details below:

University:		
Title: (eg BA Joint Hons, MA, PhD		
Subject(s):		
Year when course started:		
Year when course finished or is expected to finish:		
Full- or part-time study? (Please tick)	Full-time Part-time	Full-time Part-time
Have you obtained this degree yet? (Please tick)	Yes No	Yes No
Class: (if applicable)		

Q.12 Please give details below of any language courses you taken at the **initiative or suggestion** of your present or previous employers:

Language:				
Year started:				
Duration:				
Was the course full- or part-time? (Please tick)	Full-time Part-time	Full-time Part-time	Full-time Part-time	Full-time Part-time
If part-time, please give hours per week:				
Did you study during working time?	Yes No	Yes No	Yes No	Yes No
If studied abroad, please state country:				
Institution attended at home or abroad:				
Form of study: (eg language laboratory; classes; radio/TV programme)				
If you aimed at a formal qualification, please state which: (if none, please write NONE)				
Did you obtain this qualification? (Please tick)	Yes No	Yes No	Yes No	Yes No

74

Q.13 Please give details below of **all other** foreign language study you have undertaken whether leading to a qualification or not:

Language:				
Year started:				
Duration:				
Did you study full- or part-time? (Please tick)	Full-time ☐ Part-time ☐	Full-time ☐ Part-time ☐	Full-time ☐ Part-time ☐	Full-time ☐ Part-time ☐
If part-time, please give hours per week:				
Did you study during working time? (Please tick)	Yes ☐ No ☐	Yes ☐ No ☐	Yes ☐ No ☐	Yes ☐ No ☐
If studied abroad, please give country:				
Institution attended at home or abroad:				
Form of study: (eg language laboratory; classes; radio/TV programme)				
If you aimed at a formal qualification, please state which: (If none, please write NONE).				
Did you obtain this qualification? (please tick)	Yes ☐ No ☐	Yes ☐ No ☐	Yes ☐ No ☐	Yes ☐ No ☐

Q.14 Please give details of periods of residence abroad for three months or more in non-English speaking countries:

Country:			
Language(s)			
Year residence started:			
Duration:			
Purpose of residence:			
Was the progress you made in the command of the language of the country of residence . . .	Nil ☐ Slight ☐ Considerable ☐ Very great ☐	Nil ☐ Slight ☐ Considerable ☐ Very great ☐	Nil ☐ Slight ☐ Considerable ☐ Very great ☐

QUESTIONS 15 TO 21 ARE ABOUT THE USE MADE OF YOUR LANGUAGE SKILLS IN EMPLOYMENT

Q.15 When you **began to consider** applying for your first full-time post after graduation, did you **want** to obtain a post where you could use your language skills? (Please tick)   Yes ☐   No ☐

Q.17 If yes, did you **in fact** use these skills in this post? (Please tick)   Yes ☐   No ☐

Q.18 If Yes, please outline how you used them:

Q.19 Please indicate below all full-time posts in which you have used any of your language skills:

Starting Date	Finishing Date	Post	Languages: (please indicate whether: Essential – E / Useful – U / Occasionally Useful – O)
EXAMPLE 1968	1970	SCHOOL-TEACHER	FRENCH (E) GERMAN (E) SPANISH (O)

LEVELS OF LANGUAGE ABILITY

A. CONVERSATION

Level 1 **Understanding the spoken language:** Ability to understand a native speaker in simple conversational situations on everyday matters familiar to both parties; ability to master telephone procedure with comprehension of numerals.

Speaking: Ability to carry on simple conversation, although expressed imperfectly, on every day matters familiar to both parties; ability to issue set instructions learned in advance, telephone operating, making announcements on PA system.

Level 2 **Understanding the spoken language:** Ability to understand a native speaker at normal speed in general conversation
Speaking: Ability to carry on a conversation quite fluently, although not necessarily completely accurately, on most topics of general conversation.

Level 3 **Speaking and understanding the spoken language:** Ability to converse with ease on any subject and to understand films, radio programmes and telephone conversations almost as in the speaker's native language.

Level 4 Ability to converse as in the speaker's native language.

B. INTERPRETING
Level 1 Not applicable in this case.

Level 2 Ability to interpret **from** the foreign language **only,** a sentence at a time and within a limited range of subject matter, given adequate preparation.

Level 3 Ability to undertake occasional interpreting from the foreign language in units of two to three sentences within previously defined ranges of subject matter; and with less confidence, from English **into** the foreign language.

Level 6 Ability to undertake (a) *ad hoc* interpreting from and into the foreign language without notes, in units of two to three sentences, and/or (b) conference interpreting ie consecutive, simultaneous or whispered interpreting, usually from the foreign language **only,** of speeches and discussions at meetings normally of more than five participants.

C. READING
Level 1 Ability to read (with the aid of a dictionary) routine business communications and routine sales and technical literature.

Level 2 Ability to read (with only occasional use of a dictionary) literature within the reader's specialized field.

Level 3 Ability to read with ease almost as in the reader's native language; this pre-supposes a knowledge of the institutions and culture of the country concerned.

Level 4 Ability to read as in the reader's native language.

D. WRITING
Level 1 Ability to write (with the aid of a dictionary) only stereotyped routine letters using a very limited vocabulary.

Level 2 Ability to write (with the occasional use of a dictionary) personal letters and simple descriptive matter without gross error.

Level 3 Ability to write competently, almost as in the writer's native. This pre-supposes a knowledge of the institutions and culture of the country concerned.

Level 4 Ability to write as in the writer's native language.

E. WRITTEN TRANSLATION
Note: Translators may be called upon to translate both from and into the foreign language. The following definitions refer to translation FROM the foreign language ONLY, in accordance with recommended professional practice.
Level 1 Ability to translate (with the aid of a dictionary) **from** the foreign language, routine business communications.

Level 2 Ability to translate (with the occasional use of the dictionary) from the foreign language, literature within the translator's own specialized field,

Level 3 Ability to translate with ease **from** the foreign language, in a wide range of subject matter.

Level 4 Ability to translate **from** the foreign language, with ease on a wide range of subjects including colloquial and specialist technical material.

12. INTERVIEWS

1. Definition

'This is a scientific process of investigation using verbal communication for the purpose of collecting information with a specific aim.' (Pinto and Grawitz, 1964)

2. Principles and classification

By means of interviewing techniques it is possible to collect information on people's attitudes, impressions and ideas. As regards the individual who is expressing himself it is necessary that one or more of the following conditions by fulfilled:
– he must be able to appreciate that what he is about to say will be capable of bringing about a desired change;
– he must realize that the interviewer or the body sending the interviewer is in a position to bring about that change;
– he must perceive in the interview a means of expressing himself.
There are six types of interview that may be considered:

Non-directive interview

This method consists in suggesting a subject for the interview, the role of the interviewer being to enable the interviewee to express all that he wishes to say on the subject. There is no preliminary structure of either the discussion or the situation.

Exploratory interview

The interviewer's attitude is non-directive, but when the interviewee touches on certain important subjects he explores the field in greater detail.

Figure 7

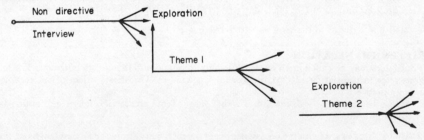

Associative interview

The individual is asked to associate freely everything that comes into his mind on a given subject.

Retrospective interview

The interview is centred essentially on past events connected with the individual.

Disturbed interview

The important feature of this type of interview is anything that interrupts the thread of the conversation (laughter, tears). Such interruptions may also be provoked by suggesting to the individual that the conversation be edited, that he should look backwards, and so on.

Centred interview

The interviewer puts definite questions which the individual has to answer. The information is quick, selectively chosen and easy to use but not of any depth.

These techniques progress from the least structuring to the most structuring.

3. Principles of construction

Similar to a questionnaire but does not go beyond macrostructurization (see questionnaire).

4. Application*

Where the aim is to work out a learner-centred method of teaching the interview is a privileged way of collecting information on attitudes, opinions, needs etc. It also forms a start to negotiation between the learner and a teaching establishment.

(See example below in *Appendix V*)

---

* *cf* – Billiez, J, *et al* (1975) *Etude de la demande de formation en langue étrangère de la population adulte de l'agglomération grenobloise.*

APPENDIX V: GUIDE D'ENTRETIEN À L'USAGE DES RESPONSABLES DE FORMATION EN LANGUES ÉTRANGÈRES

(From Billiez, J, *et al* (1975) *Etude de la demande de formation en langue étrangère de la population adulte de l'agglomération grenobloise* Vol 2, Annexes, pp 23–24)

PRESENTATION DE NOTRE RECHERCHE

L'Université des Langues et Lettres a créé un *centre de recherche* dans le domaine de la *didactique des langues étrangères* composé de linguistes, psychologues, sociologues . . .. Le centre réalise des recherches scientifiques destinées à améliorer la qualité et le rendement de l'enseignement des langues vivantes. Dans cette perspective nous effectuons à l'heure actuelle une étude, *à l'échelle régionale,* sur les motivations des adultes en langues vivantes.

1. – Pourquoi l'organisme a-t-il choisi d'enseigner les langues?
   – Depuis combien de temps cet organisme fonctionne-t-il?
   – Comment sont organisés les cours de langues? (niveau, spécialisation, matériel, cycles, groupes. . .)
   – Quelles langues sont enseignées et pourquoi?
   – Y-a-t-il un programme, une assiduité demandée, des diplômes décernés?
   – Quel est le type de pédagogie adoptée face aux adultes?

2. **Le public:**
   Qui est intéressé par ces cours, et pourquoi?
   – Comment les méthodes sont-elles ressenties par les adultes?
   – Quelles sont les difficultés ou facilités des adultes en situation d'apprentissage?
   – Les cours sont-ils suivis régulièrement? Y-a-t-il de nombreux abandons? Fournissent-ils beaucoup de travail personnel? Pourquoi veulent-ils apprendre une langue?

3. L'organisme fonctionne-t-il avec la loi de 1971 sur la Formation Permanente?
   – Comment sont recrutés les enseignants, (diplômes, nationalité française ou étrangère)?
   – Quel est le rôle des enseignants?
   – Quels sont les tarifs?
   – Quelles relations entretient-il avec son public?
   – Peuvent-ils nous fournir de la documentation ou du matériel?
   – Est-il possible d'avoir un entretien avec des personnes qui suivent des cours?

13. ATTITUDE SCALES

1. Definition

An attitude may be defined both from the cognitive and the affective point of view. An attitude is the organization of knowledge relating to one or more subjects. From the affective point of view it is a persons' predisposition to be motivated by some subject of knowledge. The scales are means of enabling people's attitudes to be displayed. The measurements they give are based on the hypothesis that attitudes can be displayed by adherence to or rejection of opinions manifested in relation to a given subject.

2. Principles and classification

2.1. Attitude and motivation

The strength of motivations depends on the state of a person's needs. Motivations appear, disappear and reappear. An attitude, on the other hand, is not bound up with a need and is therefore less specific than a motivation.

2.2. The nature of attitudes

We can distinguish five aspects:
(a) *strength* (capacity to resist any change)
(b) *magnitude* (its effect on a whole series of behaviours)
(c) *intensity* (the amount of conviction with which it is expressed)
(d) *personal commitment* with respect to the subject of the attitude
(e) *vividness* (the promptitude with which it is expressed, ease of evocation)

2.3. Constituents of the attitude

An attitude has three constituents:
– direction (attraction or repulsion);
– intensity (the attraction or repulsion are more or less marked, more or less strong);
– dimension: the object of the attitude may be simple or complex, it may be single and well defined (unidimensional attitude) or multiple (multidimensional attitude).

2.4. Attitude and opinion

An attitude is measured by adherence to or rejection of opinions which are the expression of it in words.

Both have direction, intensity and dimension.

3. Principles of construction:

There are usually said to be six stages in the construction of attitude scales:

3.1. Drafting of opinions

A maximum number (say a hundred) opinions are collected on the subject of the attitude it is desired to study. These opinions must relate to the present, avoid discussing facts and not lend themselves to interpretation in several ways. It is essential to avoid opinions that everybody can agree with and simple, direct language should be used. Words such as all, always, never, none, only and solely should be avoided.

3.2. Evaluation of opinions by a panel

A panel of people is asked to assess the opinion, ie to put it into the right perspective (as to whether it is negative or positive in relation to the subject of the attitude).

3.3. Study of marks given by the panel to the various opinions

The number of marks given to an opinion is determined by calculating the average and standard deviation of the marks awarded by the panel.

3.4. Making up the scale

The most characteristic opinions (positive, neutral or negative) are taken.

3.5. Grading of the scale

As with all measuring instruments there is the problem of accuracy and validity.

3.6. Editing

4. Application*

Attitude scales should be used whenever a problem of motivation arises. For example, the introduction of some teaching material will be all the more fruitful and appreciated if the attitude of the learners towards it is known.

(See examples below in *Appendices VI, VII and VIII*)

---

* *cf* – Gardner, R C, and W E Lambert (1972) *Attitudes and motivation in second-language learning.*
    – Jakobovits, L A (1970) *Foreign language learning: A psycholinguistic analysis of the issues.*

APPENDIX VI: FRENCH
ATTITUDE SCALE

(From Jakobovits, L A (1970) *Foreign language learning: A psycholinguistic analysis of the issues* pp 262–4)

The following statements are ones with which many people agree, and many people disagree. There are no right or wrong answers since many people have different opinions. Please indicate your agreement or disagreement by writing on the line preceding each statement the number from the following scale which best describes your feelings:

+1 slight support, agreement
+2 moderate support, agreement
+3 strong support, agreement

−1 slight opposition, disagreement
−2 moderate opposition, disagreement
−3 strong opposition, disagreement

—— 1. The French who have moved to this country have made a great contribution to the richness of our society.
—— 2. The more I get to know French-speaking people, the more I want to be able to speak their language.
—— 3. French-speaking people are very democratic in their politics and philosophy.
—— 4. French-speaking people have produced outstanding artists and writers.
—— 5. By bringing the old French folkways to our society, they have contributed greatly to our way of life.
—— 6. French-speaking people's undying faith in their religious beliefs is a positive force in this modern world.
—— 7. The French-speaking person has every reason to be proud of his race and his traditions.
—— 8. If Canada should lose the influence of French-speaking people, it would indeed be a deep loss.
—— 9. French-speaking peoples are much more polite than many Canadians.
—— 10. We can learn better ways of cooking, serving food, and entertaining from the French-speaking people.
—— 11. French-speaking people are very dependable.
—— 12. Canadian children can learn much of value by associating with French-speaking playmates.
—— 13. French-speaking people set a good example for us by their family life.
—— 14. French-speaking people are generous and hospitable to strangers.
—— 15. Canadians should make a greater effort to meet more French-speaking people.
—— 16. It is wrong to try to force the French-speaking person to become completly Canadian in his habits.
—— 17. If I had my way, I would rather live in France than in this country.
—— 18. London would be a much better city if more French-speaking people would move here.
—— 19. The French-speaking people show great understanding in the way they adjust to the Canadian way of life.
—— 20. In general, Canadian industry tends to benefit from the employment of French-speaking people.

APPENDIX VII: ÉCHELLE D'ATTITUDE À L'ÉGARD DE L'APPRENTISSAGE DES LANGUES (MAI 1977)

(Jean-Louis Chancerel et René Richterich *Séminaire de psychologie et de pédagogie, Université de Neuchâtel*)

	OUI	?	NON
1. Maintenant, il est nécessaire de connaître au moins deux langues.			
2. C'est dans la mesure où tous les habitants de la terre parleront la même langue que l'on aura enfin une paix durable.			
3. C'est un devoir pour l'école de préparer les individus à parler correctement une langue étrangère.			
4. Il faudrait organiser beaucoup plus de cours de langues pour les travailleurs immigrants afin de faciliter leur intégration dans la population.			
5. Apprendre une langue étrangère coûte cher.			
6. Apprendre une langue étrangère est difficile.			
7. C'est bon pour les gens d'un certain niveau social d'apprendre les langues étrangères.			
8. Il est plus facile d'apprendre les langues étrangères dans un pays comme la Suisse où coexistent plusieurs langues nationales.			
9. Je préférerais apprendre l'anglais plutôt que le russe; l'anglais me semble plus facile.			
10. Aujourd'hui, il est nécessaire pour tout le monde de connaître l'anglais.			
11. L'allemand devrait être une langue internationale au même titre que l'anglais et le français.			
12. Le progrès le plus significatif pour l'humanité serait l'abolition des frontières politiques et linguistiques.			
13. Etre bilingue est un atout majeur dans notre société.			
14. Les bilingues ont généralement des problèmes d'adaptation.			
15. Un bilingue n'as pas de langue maternelle.			
16. De toute façon, il est impossible de parler correctement une langue étrangère.			
17. Pour bien apprendre une langue étrangère, il faut aller dans le pays où on la parle.			
18. Je n'hésite pas à aller dans un pays où l'on parle une langue que je ne connais pas.			
19. Ce n'est pas la peine d'apprendre une langue étrangère, le language des gestes suffit souvent largement.			
20. On peut apprendre une langue étrangère sans suivre de cours.			
21. Rien ne váut de lire SHAKESPEARE dans le texte original.			
22. Traduire, c'est trahir!			
23. Savoir les langues est un signe d'intelligence.			
24. La tour de BABEL a été la première catastrophe mondiale.			
25. Après 16 ans, il est beaucoup plus difficile d'apprendre une langue.			
26. Je peux affirmer que je lis couramment un journal dans une langue étrangère.			
27. Ne pas savoir la langue dans un pays est un handicap majeur.			
28. Je pourrais travailler dans un pays où l'on parle une autre langue.			
29. Je suis gêné(e) quand des personnes parlent devant moi dans une langue que je ne comprends pas.			

APPENDIX VIII: ÉCHELLE D'ATTITUDE À L'ÉGARD DE L'ESPAGNOL (MAI 1977)

(A Bolay, S Tilbury and N Bovet
Séminaire de psychologie et de pédagogie,
Université de Neuchâtel)

	OUI	?	NON
1. Les Suisses devraient faire un plus grand effort pour rencontrer des espagnols.			
2. La vie familiale est plus importante pour les Suisses qu'elle ne l'est pour les Espagnols.			
3. Comparés aux Espagnols, les Suisses sont plus sincères et honnêtes.			
4. J'étudie l'espagnol parce que la connaissance de deux langues fera de moi une personne plus instruite.			
5. J'étudie l'espagnol parce qu'on a besoin de bien connaître au moins une langue étrangère pour mériter une certaine place dans la société.			
6. L'Espagnol a toutes les raisons d'être fier de sa nation et des ses traditions.			
7. En introduisant leurs vieilles coutumes populaires, les Espagnols ont grandement contribué à notre manière de vivre.			
8. Peu d'universités espagnoles peuvent égaler le niveau intellectuel des universités suisses.			
9. Plus j'ai l'occasion de connaître des Espagnols, plus j'aimerais être capable de parler leur langue.			
10. Les Suisses apprécient et comprennent l'art mieux que la plupart des Espagnols.			
11. Il est faux d'essayer de contraindre un Espagnol à devenir suisse dans ses habitudes.			
12. Les Espagnols naturalisés suisses contribuent à la richesse de notre société.			

14. INTELLIGENCE TESTS

We have grouped all kinds of intelligence tests (tests of intelligence, interests and personality) under this heading.

1. Definition

'The term intelligence test is used to describe a standardized experimental situation serving as a stimulus to behaviour. This behaviour is evaluated by comparing it statistically with that of other individuals placed in the same situtation, thus enabling us to classify the individual examined either quantitatively or typologically'. (Pichot)

2. Principles and classification

The definition involves four conditions:
– an experimental situation;
– registration of behaviour;
– statistical comparison;
– a reference group.

Like all measuring instruments intelligence tests must have the following qualities; accuracy, sensitivity, validity and capability of being generalized.

Classification:

– battery scales;
– sensory tests (sight, hearing, etc);
– motor and sensorimotor tests;
– attention tests;
– observation tests;
– tests of understanding and memory;
– perception, visualization and imagination tests;
– verbal capacity tests;
– tests of character and affectivity.

3. Principle of construction

In the first place a draft test is constructed that is capable of measuring a given aspect of mental attitude. This is set for a group of individuals (sample). In this way the test is graded by determining its validity, accuracy, sensitivity and capability of being generalized.

4. Application*

As a rule use will be made of tests found in commerce. With regard to these it is essential to avoid two equally dangerous attitudes: total exclusion ('intelligence tests

---

* *cf* – Wechsler, D (1955) *Manual for the Wechsler Adult Intelligence Scale,* The Psychological Corporation, New York.
   – Cattell, R B (1950) *Test 16 PF* Urbana Institute for Personality and Ability Testing.
   – Bonnardel, R, (1966) *Editions Scientifiques et Psychotechniques,* B53, Issy-les Moulineaux.

are of no use whatsoever, they violate people's personalities'); and total acceptance ('tests are the only instruments enabling us to measure people's mental attitudes'). They must be used in definite circumstances, with definite objectives. The information obtained will be all the more usable as we will be aware of its possibilities and limitations. These personality tests will complete the attitude scales by determining chances of success in language learning.

15. LANGUAGE TESTS

1. Definition

'A means of measuring connected with the carrying out of a test or a series of tests and based on the performance of an exactly defined task whose numerical notation conforms to precise criteria and a rigorous statistical exploitation. A test must be valid (ie, measure exactly what it is desired to measure) and accurate (ie maintain the same type of precision and produce the same type of results irrespective, for example, of the correctives used).' (Galisson, R, and D Coste (1976) *Dictionnaire de didiactique des langues,* p. 560).

2. Principles and classification

Aptitude tests

'give indications about the chances of success in learning a foreign language'. (Vallette, R M (1975) *Le test en langues étrangères,* p 12).

Proficiency level tests

'are not intended to measure the amount of knowledge acquired during one or more periods of instruction but to determine whether the knowledge a person has conforms with the requirements of a particular job or a given educational orientation'. (Vallette, R M, *op cit* p 12).

Subcategories: classification, employment, guidance and selection tests.

Attainment tests

'measure the extent to which a specific curriculum has been mastered at the end of a period of instruction regarded as a complete stage (ie by the end of a school year or on completion of compulsory education) without this measurement being necessarily based on a single course or method; the only thing that is common is the curriculum supposed to be covered during the period in question'. (Mothe, J-C (1975) *L'évaluation par les tests dans la classe de français,* p 18).

Progress tests

'like attainment tests, are based on a curriculum; but they measure the extent to which mastery has been gained of one unit of a particular course, the size of which unit may be extremely small'. (Mothe, J-C, *op cit* p 18).

3. Principles of construction

3.1. First define the objective or objectives which it is proposed to achieve.

3.2. Choose the various items comprising the test, which constitute a certain number of tasks to be performed by the individual, in such a way that they can be interpreted and answered in only one possible way.

3.3. Lay down instructions on the setting of tests so that they can be interpreted in one way only.

3.4. Prepare standardized methods of correcting, ie so that correction can take only one form.

3.5. Establish criteria for success.

3.6. Check that the test is valid (do the different items really measure what they are intended to measure, namely, the objective(s) set?) and its accuracy (do the chosen items and the methods of setting and of correcting guarantee stable, consistent results?).

4. Application*: *cf* 2.

* *cf* – *Pimsleur Language Aptitude Battery,* Form 5, (1966) Harcourt, Brace & World, New York.
  – *MLA Cooperative Foreign Language Tests,* Forms LA and MA, (1963) Princeton, Educational Testing Service.
  – *Test CGM 62* (1964) Didier.

16. JOB ANALYSIS

1. Definition

We may start from what Gillet says about the detection of needs:

'Detection of needs is based mainly on the observation of those holding the job by identifying, whether systematically or otherwise, their difficulties, mistakes, standard situations, sources of incidents, and so on. Such observation is conducted in conjunction with interviews or the setting of questionnaires for the purpose of identifying in the function, those elements which lend themselves to a process of training.' (*cf Bibliography*)

In the particular case of language-learning needs, it will be a case of getting to know whether the acquisition of a certain number of qualifications in the use of a foreign language is indispensable, necessary or desirable.

2. Principles and classification

The process of working out a programme of training for a job may be divided into seven stages:

– analysis of the operational sub-system. This means determining all the procedures used at factory, workshop or group level (selection, job enrichment, etc);
– analysis of a particular job:
  – situating the job in the sub-system;
  – specifying the necessary knowledge and qualifications;
  – detecting the proficiency standards to be used for the purpose of validating the training programme processes;
  – converting the necessary knowledge and qualifications into more general terms (key qualifications, basic psychological processes, types of learning, etc);
  – laying down the objectives of the training;
  – restating the proficiency standards;
  – assessing the value of the training programme.

Job analysis methods may be classified as follows:

– analysis of work in terms of time and elementary movements (manual jobs);
– analysis in terms of communication
  – analysis of work signals;
  – men/machines systems;
– Flanagan's critical incident technique (*cf Bibliography*);
– analysis of mistakes made in connection with the work;
– analysis of the terms of qualification;
– sociological and technical analysis of work situations.

3. Principles of construction

Job analysis consists of the following stages:

– locating the job in its environment (economic, social and material);
– collecting information about the job;

– summarizing this information in terms of job description;
– deciding on what training is needed.

4. Application*

Wherever language learning is linked to a job.

---

* cf Bung, K, (1973) *The foreign language needs of waiters and hotel staff*, Council of Europe, Strasbourg, mimeograph.

17. CONTENT ANALYSIS

1. Definition

'The totality of techniques designed to reveal in the content of different categories of written background material (newspaper articles, interviews, questionnaires, personal notes, etc) certain specific elements from which we then derive some psycho-sociological characterization of the individuality under consideration' (Gardin)

2. Principles of classification

The aim of content analysis is to bring out the signifiers contained in the text studied. It is necessary to proceed from rough data (speech) to a model (hypotheses, speech structure, compositions, etc) taking account of them in a synthetic manner.

Thematic content analyses (the different themes covered in a talk are singled out) may also be contrasted with *structural* content analyses (the structures in the talk are singled out). It is also possible to distinguish such analyses according to their reference models (psychoanalysis, structuralism, Marxism, etc).

In any event the content analysis refers to the WHAT of the communication (WHO says WHAT to WHOM with WHAT EFFECT). We can then subscribe to Berelson's definition: (*cf Bibliography*)

'It is a method of research whose aim is an objective, systematic and quantitative description of the content of the communication.'

Thus we see that there are three requirements – the analysis must be *objective*, *systematic* and *quantitative*.

3. Principles of construction

We can describe seven stages in content analysis:
– collecting all the data (exhaustive character of the conversation(s));
– defining the content unit that can be isolated and has significance;
– selecting the variables;
– classifying the variables;
– finding the links between the variables;
– establishing the structure of the links between the variables;
– constructing a model.

The problems that arise are thus essentially problems of units (from words to paragraphs) of criteria for the selection of categories, of methods of processing the data and of interpretation of the results.

4. Application*

Content analysis may be used wherever a talk or conversation has to be dealt with. It will relate to material collected by the method of interviews or from existing textbooks.

---

* *cf* James, C V, and S Rouve (1973) *Survey of curricula and performance in modern languages.*

18. STATISTICS

1. Definition

Methods of processing numerical data are called statistics.

2. Principles and classification

The processing is linked to the level of measurement and to the capabilities of dealing with the data:

manual processing;
mechanical processing;
processing by computer.

The use of a computer is necessary whenever the number of subjects is greater than 120 and the number of variables exceeds ten.

3. Application*

Whenever we have to deal with numerical data. For anything beyond elementary statistics (percentages, averages, and so on) we have to use a data-processing specialist.

---

* *cf* Österreichisches Statistisches Zentralamt (1976) *Fremdsprachenkenntnisse der österreichischen Bevölkerung*.

19. DETERMINATION OF OBJECTIVES

1. Definition

'An objective is an intent communicated by a statement describing a proposed change in a learner – a statement of what the learner is to be like when he has successfully completed a learning experience. It is a description of a pattern of behaviour (performance) we want the learner to be able to demonstrate.' (Mager, R F, *Preparing instructional objectives*, p 3)

2. Principles and classification:

It is always advisable to indicate precisely at what level the objectives are to be defined:

(a) *Long-term:*
 – general objectives;
 – operational objectives.
(b) *Short-term:*
 – general objectives;
 – operational objectives

and in what terms:

– phonetics, morphology, syntax, lexis;
– referential objects;
– language activities, functions, situations;
– understanding speech and speaking;
– reading and writing.

3. Principles of construction:

An objective consists of:
– an action;
– a content;
– a situation of use;
– achievement criteria.

'Laying down learning objectives therefore means answering a series of questions:
 ● What will be the learner's status, roles and characteristics as a speaker of the foreign language?
 ● With what sort of people (status, roles, characteristics) will he have to communicate?
 ● What speech acts will he have to be able to accomplish and in reaction to what other acts?
 ● In what situations will he have to carry out these acts?
 ● In reference to which fields of experience will the language exchanges take place?' (Coste, D, *et al* (1976) *Un niveau-seuil* p 17)

4. Application*

Specifying jointly with the learners what their objectives are as determined by pre-prepared lists.

---

* *cf* van Ek, J (1975) *The Threshold Level* Council of Europe, Strasbourg and Pergamon Press, Oxford, 1980.
Coste, D, *et al* (1976) *Un niveau-seuil* Council of Europe, Strasbourg.
SKF stages of attainment scale (1975) English Language Teaching Development Unit and Oxford University Press, Colchester.

Discussing with them the definition of those objectives.

Making discussion and definition of objectives an integral part of the teaching material.

(See examples below in *Appendices IX, X* and *XI*)

APPENDIX IX: DÉFINIR LES OBJECTIFS DE L'ÉDUCATION

(V and G de Landesheere, p 26)

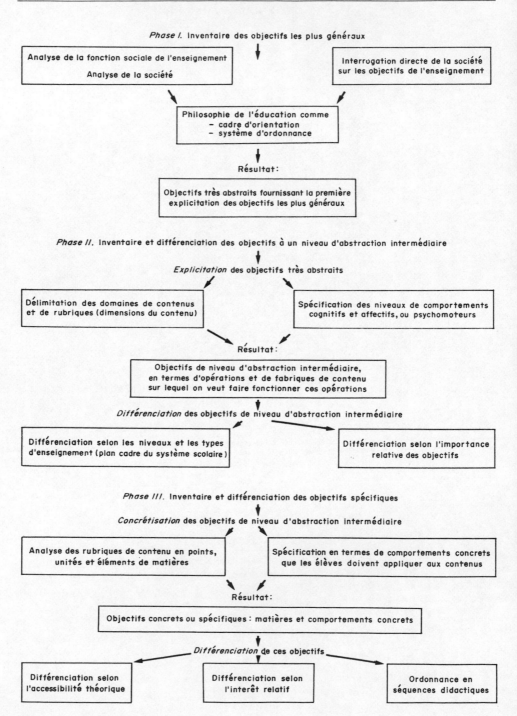

Phase I. Inventaire des objectifs les plus généraux

Analyse de la fonction sociale de l'enseignement

Analyse de la société

Interrogation directe de la société sur les objectifs de l'enseignement

Philosophie de l'éducation comme
– cadre d'orientation
– système d'ordonnance

Résultat:

Objectifs très abstraits fournissant la première explicitation des objectifs les plus généraux

Phase II. Inventaire et différenciation des objectifs à un niveau d'abstraction intermédiaire

Explicitation des objectifs très abstraits

Délimitation des domaines de contenus et de rubriques (dimensions du contenu)

Spécification des niveaux de comportements cognitifs et affectifs, ou psychomoteurs

Résultat:

Objectifs de niveau d'abstraction intermédiaire, en termes d'opérations et de fabriques de contenu sur lequel on veut faire fonctionner ces opérations

Différenciation des objectifs de niveau d'abstraction intermédiaire

Différenciation selon les niveaux et les types d'enseignement (plan cadre du système scolaire)

Différenciation selon l'importance relative des objectifs

Phase III. Inventaire et différenciation des objectifs spécifiques

Concrétisation des objectifs de niveau d'abstraction intermédiaire

Analyse des rubriques de contenu en points, unités et éléments de matières

Spécification en termes de comportements concrets que les élèves doivent appliquer aux contenus

Résultat:

Objectifs concrets ou spécifiques: matières et comportements concrets

Différenciation de ces objectifs

Différenciation selon l'accessibilité théorique

Différenciation selon l'intérêt relatif

Ordonnance en séquences didactiques

APPENDIX X: THE LONDON CHAMBER OF COMMERCE AND INDUSTRY, p 2

Language activities
Reading reports/correspondence
Conversation with one person
Use of telephone
Travelling abroad
Receiving and entertaining foreign visitors
Informal meeting with two to five people
Writing letters
Being entertained abroad
Writing telegrams, telex, etc
Reading technical journals/newspapers
Understanding discussions at formal meetings
Reading instruction manuals/brochures
Listening to conference, speeches, lectures, etc
Writing sales leaflets/instruction brochures
Speaking at formal meetings
Giving instructions and training
Taking notes at meetings/conferences
Writing reports and minutes
Following a training course
Chairing meetings/conferences
Foreign language shorthand

APPENDIX XI: PROSPECTUS DES EUROCENTRES

De quoi serez-vous capable dans la langue étrangère?

PROSPECTUS DES EUROCENTRES

Les indications suivantes donnent un aperçu général de ce que vous pouvez espérer apprendre aux différents niveaux

Le point de départ
c'est-à-dire le niveau initial de votre groupe, est déterminé par les résultats du test passé à l'arrivée

Nous estimons qu'un étudiant motivé et travailleur a besoin, en règle générale, de trois mois pour réaliser dans a langue étrangère les différentes fonctions définies à chaque niveau.

Les détails du programme, l'étendue et la solidité des aptitudes que vous pouvez acquérir, dépendent du type de cours choisi et de sa durée. Toutefois, vos dispositions pour les langues, votre motivation et votre empressement à utiliser toutes les ressources du milieu pèseront d'un poids égal dans votre réussite finale.

Niveau débutant et élémentaire
Vous vous initiez au maniement des structures grammaticales de base et vous vous exercez à parler. Vous vous entraînez à comprendre et à employer un vocabulaire fondamental dans les situations de tous les jours. Vous apprenez, notamment, à utiliser convenablement la langue pour
- vous présenter et indiquer votre profession ou vos occupations habituelles;
- faire état de vos besoins, de vos goûts et de vos aversions;
- poser des questions sur ces sujets;
- obtenir des renseignements;
- obtenir qu'on fasse certaines choses pour vous;
- formuler une demande, une suggestion ou une invitation dans des situations de la vie quotidienne;

- formuler une proposition ou y répondre; vous excuser selon les règles de la politesse;
- donner des instructions simples ou réagir à une mise en garde;
- comprendre les inscriptions, les écriteaux et annonces à l'usage du public;
- déchiffrer et écrire des messages simples;
- rendre compte de vive voix ou par écrit d'une action passée;
- indiquer verbalement ou par écrit ce que vous êtes sur le point de faire

Niveau intermédiaire
Vous consolidez vos acquis, tout en accroissant l'aisance et la justesse de votre expression. En outre, vous apprenez à
- parler et écrire sur vous-même et sur ce qui vous entoure;
- décrire ce que vous avez vu;
- comprendre une conversation courante menée à un débit normal;
- prendre part à une conversation;
- donner des instructions ou indiquer un mode d'emploi;
- lire des informations ou vous exprimer par écrit sur des sujets courants;
- exprimer votre opinion;
- exprimer votre accord ou désaccord, votre approbation ou désapprobation;
- écrire des lettres simples;
- transmettre fidèlement une information;
- communiquer par téléphone.

Niveau moyen
Complétant les bases solides que vous avez déjà acquises, vous apprenez à vous exprimer avec justesse et naturel dans la plupart de situations. Vous êtes, notamment, e mesure de
- engager une conversation,
- soutenir une idée et défendre votr point de vue;
- comprendre une information écrite, sur tout sujet d'intérêt général, tel qu'un article de journal, message publicitaire ou publication officielle;
- saisir le sens exact de ce qui est énoncé oralement, enregistré ou radiodiffusé, sur tout sujet d'intérêt général;
- énoncer des avis critiques, verbalement ou par écrit;
- rédiger un rapport;
- exprimer un désir ou une intentio verbalement ou par écrit;
- rédiger une lettre administrative pour les autorités.

Niveau avancé
A ce stade, vous vous exprimez avec assurance, utilisant le mot juste et le nuances de la langue étrangère pour traduire votre personnalité. Vous êtes capable, notamment, de
- développer, de vive voix ou par écrit, un raisonnement sur des sujets abstraits;
- participer, dans la conversation o en débat public, à la discussion de sujets divers de caractère social, culturel ou professionnel;
- prendre des notes, rédiger un rapport, résumer par écrit un discours ou une conférence;
- comprendre le sens exact de texte se rapportant à votre vie professionnelle ou personnelle,
- faire une causerie sur un sujet préparé à l'avance;
- résumer oralement ou par écrit u article ou un rapport.

BIBLIOGRAPHY

1. Surveys and analyses

Ahlquist, P (nd) *Knowledge of English among Swedes. An investigation made in 1967.* Duplicated.

AKS *Ergebnisse der Fragebogenaktion zur Ermittlung des Sprachlernbedarfs an Hochschulen der BRD durchgeführt aufgrund der Beschlüsse der AKS-Arbeitstagung in Tübingen am 10–11. Oktober, 1972. 4. Arbeitstagung des AKS vom 27–29. September, 1973 in Trier.* Duplicated.

Bibeau, G et al (1976) *Rapport de l'etude indépendante sur les programmes de formation linguistique de la fonction publique du Canada.* Commission de la Fonction publique, Ottawa, 12 vols.

Billiez, J, et al (1975) *Etude de la demande de formation en langue étrangère de la population adulte de l'agglomération grenobloise* Université des langues et lettres, Centre de didactique des langues, service de l'éducation permanent, Grenoble, 2 vols.

Bourgoz, R, et al (1971) *Quelques aspects de l'éducation permanent en Suisse. Enquête sur les motivations de fréquentation des cours para-professionnels chez les adultes, effectuée dans un centre-test de formation: l'Ecole-Club Migros de Lausanne* Institut d'études sociales, Genève.

Chancerel, J-L, and A Sipitanou (nd) *Apprentissage des langues par les adultes. Enquête du Conseil de l'Europe, Questionnaire de Saint-Wolfgang* (EES/Symposium 57,2, 1972, Conseil de l'Europe) Conseil de l'Europe et Séminaire de psychologie de l'Université de Neuchâtel, Strasbourg et Neuchâtel. Duplicated.

CREDIF (1976) *Analyses des besoins langagiers d'adultes en milieu professionnel (préalables d'une formation)* CREDIF, Saint-Cloud. Duplicated ENS.

Deutscher Volkshochschul-Verband (1968) *Das Angebot berufsbezogener Bildung. Ergebnisse einer Auswertung der VHS-Arbeitspläne.* Pädagogische Arbeitsstelle, Frankfurt. Duplicated.

Deutscher Volkhochschul-Verband (1968) *Berichte aus der Praxis der VHS-Organisation. (Auswertung einer Umfrage bei Volkshochschulen).* Pädagogische Arbeitsstelle, Frankfurt. Duplicated.

Deutscher Volkhochschul-Verband (1976) *Unterlagen zur Konferenz 'Bedarfanalyse im Sprachenbereich'.* Pädagogische Arbeitsstelle, Frankfurt. Duplicated.

Dittrich, A W (1975) *Umfrage zu den Lernziel-Katalogen der Gutachterkommission Lernziele.* Goethe-Institut, München. Duplicated.

Emmans, K, E Hawkins and A Westoby (1974) *Foreigh languages in industry/commerce.* University of York, Language Teaching Centre.

English Language Teaching Development Unit (Oxford University Press) (1970) *English for Business.* Prepared for English by Radio and Television (British Broadcasting Corporation). I. Research and Preliminary Planning Report. ELTDU, Colchester. Duplicated.

Evans, G, and E Pastor (1972) *Communication 12 1/2, Field survey of language skills and real job needs.* SIDA, Stockholm. Duplicated.

Ford (1976) *Der Pilotlehrgang: Deutsch am laufenden Band.* Bildungszentrum der Ford-Werke Aktiengesellschaft, Köln.

Ford (1973) *Bedarfsanalyse Englisch.* Bildungszentrum der Ford-Werke Aktiengesellschaft, Köln.

Kilian, V (1975) *Materialien zur Auswertung der Umfrage. Fragebogen zum Stand des betrieblichen Sprachunterrichts und zur Entwicklung des Bedarfs an Fremdsprachenqualifikation (März/April 1974).* Informationszentrum für Fremdsprachenforschung, Marburg. Duplicated.

Knab, D (1973) *Bericht für die Unterkommission 'Baukastenansatz' der Plannungskommission 'Erwachsenenbildung und Weiterbildung'.* Deutscher Volkshochschul-Verband, Pädagogische Arbeitsstelle, Frankfurt, Duplicated.

Larsson, I (1969) The German language in parts of Swedish industry and commerce. *Pedagogoical-Psychological Problems, no 101.* Institute of Education and Psychology of the College of Education, Malmö. Translated by Peter Green in 1971.

London Chamber of Commerce and Industry (nd) *Commercial Education Scheme report on the 'market survey' of the non-specialist use of foreign languages in industry and commerce.* Marlowe House, Sidcup, Kent. Duplicated.

Migros (1969) *Motivforschung 1969.* MGB-Koordinationsstelle der Klubschulen, Zürich.

Neuhaus, K (1977) Sozialdaten und Motivationsstruktur von Teilnehmern an Sprachkursen-Ergebnisse einer Umfrage. *Zielsprache Englisch,* 1 pp 33–37.

Nickel, G (1970) *Etude sur l'enseignement des langues étrangères dans les pays de langue allemande.* CCC/ESR/LV (70) 73, Council of Europe, Strasbourg. Duplicated.

Österreichisches Statistisches Zentralamt (1976) *Fremdsprachenkenntnisse der oesterreichischen Bevölkerung Ergebnisse des Mikrozensus Dezember 1974. Heft 430* Beiträge zur Österreichischen Statistik, Wien.

Riddy, D C (1973) *Analyse des réponses au questionnaire (DECS/EGT 72,4) sur l'enseignement des langues vivantes dans les Etats membres du Conseil de la Coopération Culturelle.* CCC/EGT (73) 15 Comité de l'Enseignement Général et Technique. Duplicated.

Swedish Broadcasting Corporation (nd) *Investigation among adults on their interest for courses in TV and Radio. A summary of the report 30/69.* Duplicated.

2. Generalities

Baltruweit, S (1975) *Analyse fremdsprachlicher Curricula in der Weiterbildung.* Pädagogische Arbeitsstelle des Deutschen Volkshochschul-Verbandes. Frankfurt.

Bung, K (1973) *The foreign language needs of waiters and hotel staff.* CCC/EES (73) 19, Council of Europe, Strasbourg. Duplicated.

Chancerel, J-L, et al (1975) *Adult education 'needs'; methods of identifying them.* CCC/EES (75) 20, Council of Europe, Strasbourg. Duplicated.

Coste, D, et al. (1976) *Un niveau-seuil.* Council of Europe, Strasbourg.

van Ek, J (1975) *The threshold level.* Council of Europe, Strasbourg, and Pergamon Press, Oxford, 1980.

Ferenczi, V (1976) Les besoins langagiers comme représentation des pratiques sociales d'intercommunication. *Revue de Phonétique Appliquée.* Université de l'Etat de Mons, no 38, pp. 81–94.

Galisson, R, and D Coste, (1976) *Dictionnaire de didactique des langues.* Hachette, Paris.

Hondrich, K O (1975) *Menschliche Bedürfnisse und soziale Steuerung.* Rowohlt, RORORO Studium, Reinbeck bei Hamburg.

James, C V, and S Rouve (1973) *Survey of Curricula and Performance in Modern Languages 1971–1972.* Centre for Information on Language Teaching and Research.

James, C V (1974) 'Estimating adult needs' in: *Teaching Languages to adults for special purposes.* (CILT Reports and Papers 11). Centre for Information on Language Teaching and Research, pp 76–90.

Mareschal, R (*ed*) (1977) Besoins langagiers et enseignement des langues. *La Revue Canadienne des Langues Vivantes.* Vol 33, no 5, mai.

Porcher, L (1977) Une notion ambiguë: les 'besoins langagiers' (Linguistique, sociologie, pédagogie). *Les Cahiers du CRELEF,* no 3, Besançon, pp 1–12.

Richterich, R (1973) 'Definition of language needs and types of adults' in *Systems development in adult language learning.* Council of Europe, Strasbourg and Pergamon Press, Oxford, 1980

Richterich, R (1975) 'The analysis of language needs. Illusion – pretext – necessity' in 'Modern language learning by adults' *Education and Culture,* no 28. Council of Europe, Strasbourg, pp 9–14.

Richterich, R (1974) 'The analysis of languages needs' in *Modern languages in adult education.* EES/ Symposium 57, 10. Council of Europe, Strasbourg, pp 14–22. Duplicated.

Richterich, R (1973) *The role of the analysis of language needs for establishing a unit/credit system for modern language learning.* CCC/EES (73) 23, Council of Europe, Strasbourg. Duplicated.

Roulet, E (1977) *Un niveau-seuil. Presentation and guide to use.* Council of Europe, Strasbourg.

Rousson, M, and G Boudineau (1977) L'étude des besoins de formation. Réflexions théoriques et méthodologiques. *Dossiers de Psychologie,* août 1977. Centre de Psychologie, Université de Neuchâtel, Neuchâtel. Duplicated.

Systems development in adult language learning. Council of Europe, Strasbourg, 1973, and Pergamon Press, Oxford, 1980

Trim J L M (1975) 'A European unit/credit system' in 'Modern language learning by adults' *Education and Culture,* no 28. Council of Europe, Strasbourg, pp 3–8.

Wilkins, D (1975) *The general structure of a unit/credit system for modern language learning by adults: preliminary proposals.* CCC/EES (75) 55 Council of Europe, Strasbourg. Duplicated.

3. Methods

3.1. Surveys

Festinger, L, and D Katz (1963) *Les méthodes de recherche dans les sciences sociales.* Presses Universitaires de France, Paris. 2 vols.

Lewin, K (1968) *Psychologie dynamique.* Presses Universitaires de France, Paris.

3.2. Sample surveys

Desabie, J (1966) *Théorie et pratique des sondages.* Dunod, Paris.

3.3. Questionnaires

Chancerel, J-L (1969) *Méthodologie d'enquêtes en milieu rural.* Ecole nationale de la santé publique, Rennes.

Daval, R (1964) *Traité de psychologie sociale.* Presses Universitaires de France, Paris. 2 vols.

Matalon, B (1966) *L'analyse hiérarchique.* Gauthier-Villars, Paris.

3.4. Interviews

Dorra, H G, and G Millet (1970) Comment mener un entretien individuel. Dunod, Paris.

Newcomb, T, R H Turner, and P Converse (1970) *Manuel de psychologie sociale. L'interaction des individus.* Presses Universitaires de France, Paris.

Pinto, R, and M Grawitz (1964) *Méthodes dans les sciences sociales.* Dalloz, Paris.

Rogers, C R (1970) *Le développement de la personne.* Dunod, Paris.

3.5. Attitude scales

Alexandre, V (1971) *Les échelles d'attitude.* Editions Universitaires, Paris.

Debaty, P (1967) *La mesure des attitudes.* Presses Universitaires de France, Paris.

Gardner, R C, and W E Lambert (1972) *Attitudes and motivation in second-language learning.* Newbury House Publishers, Rowley.

Jakobovits, L A (1970) *Foreign language learning: A psycholinguistic analysis of the issues.* Newbury House Publishers, Rowley.

Krech, D, and R S Crachtfeld (1952) *Théorie et problèmes de psychologie sociale.* Presses Universitaires de France, Paris, 2 vols.

3.6. Intelligence tests

Albou, P (1968) *Les questionnaires psychologiques.* Presses Universitaires de France, Paris.

Pichot, P (1967) *Les tests mentaux* (Collection: Que Sais-je?). Presses Universitaires de France, Paris.

Zurfluh, J (1976) *Les tests mentaux.* Jean-Pierre Delarge, Paris.

3.7. Language tests

Buros, O K (1975) *Foreign language tests and reviews.* The Gryphon Press, Highland Park, New Jersey.

Chaplen, E F (1975) *Measuring achievement in adult language learning.* CCC/EES (75) 73. Council of Europe, Strasbourg. Duplicated.

Clark, J L D (1972) *Foreign language testing: theory and practice.* The Centre for Curriculum Development, Philadelphia.

Fehse, K-D, and W Praeger (1973) *Bibliographie zum Testen in der Schule. Schwerpunkt: Fremdsprache.* Universitätsverlag Becksmann, Freiburg.

Mothe, J C (1975) *L'évaluation par les tests dans la classe de français* (Collection: Le Français dans le Monde/BELC. Hachette/Larousse, Paris).

Paquette, A F, and S Tollinger (1968) *A Handbook on foreign language classroom testing: French, German, Italian, Russian, Spanish.* Modern Language Association of America, New York.
van Passel, F (1972) 'Tests d'auto-évaluation pour une langue étrangère' in *Procès-verbal de l'assemblée générale de l'AIMAV, réunion du 12 décembre 1972.* AIMAV, Brussels, pp 19–26.

Savard, J G (1969) *Bibliographie analytique de tests de langue.* Presses de l'Université Laval, Québec. Nouvelle édition 1975.

Valette, R M (1975) *Le test en langues étrangères. Guide pratique.* Classiques Hachette, Paris.
Valette, R M (1967) *Modern language testing: A handbook.* Harcourt, Brace & World, New York.

3.8. Job analysis

Flanagan, J C (1954) Technique de l'incident critique *Revue de Psychologie Appliquée.* XII, 1 and 2, pp 3–27, 7–45.

Gillet, B (1973) *Améliorer la formation professionnelle par l'étude du travail.* Les Editions d'organisation, Paris.

3.9. Content analysis

Berelson, B (1952) 'Content analysis' in Gardner and Lindsey, *Handbook of social psychology.* Wesley Publishing Company, Reading.

Gardin, J C (1974) *Les analyses de discours.* Delachaux et Niestlé, Neuchâtel.

Harris, Z S (1963) *Discourse analysis.* Mouton, The Hague.

Maingueneau, D (1976) *Initiation aux méthodes de l'analyse du discours.* Hachette Université, Paris.

d'Unrug, M C (1974) *Analyse de contenu.* Editions Universitaires, Paris.

3.10. Statistical analysis

Fischer, H (1955) *Les méthodes statistiques en psychologie et en pédagogie.* Delachaux et Niestlé, Neuchâtel.

Hays, W L, and R L Winkler (1970) *Statistics* Holt, Rinehart & Winston, New York.

3.11. The objectives

Bung, K (1973) *The specification of objectives in a language learning system for adults.* CCC/EES (73) 34. Council of Europe, Strasbourg. Duplicated.

D'Hainaut, L (1970) Un modèle pour la détermination et la sélection des objectifs pédagogiques du domaine cognitif. *Enseignement Programmé,* 11, pp 21–38.

English Language Teaching Development Unit (1975) *English language. Stages of attainment scale prepared for Aktiebolaget Svenska Kullagerfabriken.* ELTDU, Oxford University Press, Colchester.

Ford (1976) *Das neue Englisch-Sprachlehrsystem. Informationen für Berater und Management.* Bildungszentrum der Ford-Werke Aktiengesellschaft, Köln.
Freihoff, R and S Takala (1974) *A systematic description of language-teaching objectives based on the specification of language use situations.* Language Centre University Jyväskylä, Jyväskylä. Abridged version.

Germain, C (1974) *L'enseignement individualisé, l'enseignement par objectifs de comportement, et la formation des professeurs de langues. Communication faite dans le cadre du IIIe colloque SGAV.* Université d'Ottawa, Ottawa. Duplicated.

Hüllen, W *et al* (1975) *Lernzielbestimmung und Leistungsmessung im modernen Fremdsprachenunterricht.* Diesterweg, Frankfurt/Main.

IBM (1974) *Level performance charts.* Compagnie IBM France, Paris.

Landsheere de, V and G (1975) *Définir les objectifs de l'éducation.* Presses Universitaires de France, Paris.

Mager, R F (1962) *Preparing instructional objectives.* Fearon Publishers, Belmont.

Steiner, F. (1975) *Performing with objectives.* Newbury House Publishers, Rowley.

Valette, R M, and R S Disick (1972) *Modern language performance objectives and individualization. A handbook.* Harcourt Brace Jovanovich, New York.